The *Spicy* PLANT-BASED Cookbook

More Than 200 Fiery Snacks, Dips, and Main Dishes for the Plant-Based Lifestyle

Adams Media

New York   London   Toronto   Sydney   New Delhi

Adams media

Adams Media
An Imprint of Simon & Schuster, Inc.
57 Littlefield Street
Avon, Massachusetts 02322

First Adams Media trade paperback edition January 2021

ADAMS MEDIA and colophon are trademarks of Simon & Schuster.

For information about special discounts for bulk purchases, please contact Simon & Schuster Special Sales at 1-866-506-1949 or business@simonandschuster.com.

The Simon & Schuster Speakers Bureau can bring authors to your live event. For more information or to book an event contact the Simon & Schuster Speakers Bureau at 1-866-248-3049 or visit our website at www.simonspeakers.com.

Interior design by Julia Jacintho
Photographs by James Stefiuk
Illustrations © 123RF/melazerg, larysaray; Getty Images/AllNikArt

Manufactured in the United States of America

10 9 8 7 6 5 4 3 2 1

Library of Congress Cataloging-in-Publication Data
Names: Adams Media (firm).
Title: The spicy plant-based cookbook.
Description: First Adams Media trade paperback edition. | Avon, Massachusetts: Adams Media, 2021. | Includes index.
Identifiers: LCCN 2020034998 | ISBN 9781507214596 (pb) | ISBN 9781507214602 (ebook)
Subjects: LCSH: Vegetarian cooking. | Vegan cooking. | Cooking (Spices) | LCGFT: Cookbooks.
Classification: LCC TX837 .S6889 2021 | DDC 641.5/636--dc23

LC record available at https://lccn.loc.gov/2020034998

ISBN 978-1-5072-1459-6
ISBN 978-1-5072-1460-2 (ebook)

Contains material adapted from the following titles published by Adams Media, an Imprint of Simon & Schuster, Inc.: *The Spicy Vegan Cookbook* by Adams Media, copyright © 2014, ISBN 978-1-4405-7323-1; *The Spicy Vegetarian Cookbook* by Adams Media, copyright © 2014, ISBN 978-1-4405-7326-2; *The Everything® Indian Cookbook* by Monica Bhide, copyright © 2004, ISBN 978-1-59337-042-8; *The Everything® Thai Cookbook, 2nd Edition* by Jam Sanitchat, copyright © 2013, ISBN 978-1-4405-6154-2; *The Everything® Mexican Cookbook* by Margaret Kaeter, copyright © 2003, ISBN 978-1-58062-967-6.

Contents

Chapter Five
SALADS.....................................99

Chapter Six
SOUPS, STEWS, AND CHILIS......... 127

Chapter Seven
MAIN DISHES.............................. 157

Introduction

Creole Jambalaya. Chipotle–Black Bean Salad. Spiced Chocolate Cake.

Today, hot and spicy dishes like these are making their way onto vegetarian and vegan dining menus alike. Adventurous plant-based home chefs are stepping outside of their culinary comfort zones to up the heat with all-natural ingredients. And while you could just add a hot sauce on the side of your meal, there is nothing more satisfying than creating a nuanced and truly spicy plant-based meal in the comfort of your own home. Fortunately, *The Spicy Plant-Based Cookbook* offers more than two hundred delicious recipes guaranteed to give your palate the heat it's been looking for!

Here you'll learn how to incorporate spice into your meals as you perfectly balance the heat with other plant-based ingredients, creating dynamically spicy cuisine. You'll enjoy all the health benefits of a spicy plant-based diet, including lowered inflammation and all-natural plant-based nutrition without the overprocessed ingredients. The hot and spicy plant-based recipes that you'll find throughout the book range from breakfast and lunch items to snacks and desserts, so you can satisfy all your spice cravings with natural, nutritious, and meatless ingredients.

You'll also find some advice in Chapter 1 on how to incorporate the spicy plant-based diet into your life, with tips on plant-based grocery lists and shopping, meal planning, handling spices, and more. And just in case you aren't familiar with the plant-based lifestyle or common spices, you'll find some helpful tips to get you started and help you cook like a pro—from essential nutritional info to key ingredients. So get ready to embrace your new spicy plant-based lifestyle! Whether you're looking for a little extra kick or out-of-this world heat, *The Spicy Plant-Based Cookbook* provides the flamin'-hot flavor *and* the plant-based nutrition that your body wants, needs, and deserves.

Chapter One

SPICY PLANT-BASED 101

If you're the kind of person whose mouth immediately starts to water when you hear the phrase "flaming hot," but who still wants to follow a healthy, balanced diet, then eating plant-based is for you! A well-planned plant-based diet can be an easy way to get the nutrients you need, feel great every day, and still get to enjoy your favorite spicy dishes.

In this chapter, you'll learn exactly what the plant-based diet is and why it's so great for your body. You'll also see that it's fully customizable and perfect for anyone who loves to bring a little spice to their cooking and get the nutritional benefits of all kinds of peppers. It's easy to bring your plant-based cooking to the next red-hot level!

What Is the Plant-Based Diet?

At its simplest, the plant-based diet emphasizes whole, real foods from plant sources. Essentially, when eating plant-based, your meals should be focused on fresh, minimally processed foods that are complete as nature intended them. That means that your favorite spicy peppers are safe...while some of your other favorite ingredients might not be.

What to Avoid

First and foremost, you'll want to avoid eating highly processed, refined foods while on the plant-based diet. Refined foods such as sugars and flours are often stripped of their natural nutrients. Even when foods are "enriched"—which means that the nutrients lost during refining are added back in—the end product is never the same as the original whole food. Other grains may be highly processed as well. Make sure to stick with whole grains.

You'll also want to consider the amount of animal products you're consuming, since that can be a bit more controversial on the plant-based diet. While some people will choose to remove all animal products from their diet, others will cut out only meat. Others still may decide just to limit their meat intake while still consuming other animal products. When it comes to the plant-based diet, a good rule is to at least limit how much meat you eat so it's not the main focus of your meal. Instead, think of it as more of a side dish or even a condiment while you focus most of your attention on fruits, vegetables, and other healthy sources of protein.

You'll find that all the recipes in this book are completely vegetarian-friendly. However, you can easily modify the recipes to suit your personal needs. Consider adding in some natural animal products (or even a small amount of meat) if that's what keeps you feeling your best. Feel free to experiment with vegan alternatives as well. Just remember that swapping out individual ingredients will change the nutrition facts included with each recipe, so be mindful of the changes you make.

What to Include

Although the meals you'll find in this book don't include any meat or animal products, they do include a balanced variety of other fresh ingredients (and some extra spiciness!) to help make sure you get the nutrients you need. As you're preparing your food, think about how you're representing each of these major food categories:

- **Vegetables:** Vegetables are an essential part of every plant-based meal...and those delicious spicy peppers will count toward this group as well!
- **Fruit:** Fruits can be a great sweet complement to an otherwise spicy dish. Check out the salsas, salads, and desserts for ways to incorporate fruits into your spiciest dishes.
- **Whole Grains:** On the plant-based diet, it's important to avoid refined and highly processed foods, which means it's best to avoid things like white bread and white rice. Instead, look for whole-grain options, like brown rice or whole-wheat pasta to complement your dishes.
- **Protein:** Meat is generally limited or eliminated in the plant-based diet, so you'll want to make sure you have other protein sources. Beans, nuts, and other plant-based proteins are a great addition.
- **Healthy Oils/Fats:** Some healthy fats are important to include in your everyday diet. Olive oil and avocados are great examples.

When determining how best to transition to the plant-based diet, it's important to think about what works best for you and your body. You may want to consult with a professional for more advice—consider visiting your regular physician or meeting with a dietitian if you feel you need more help.

Following the Plant-Based Diet...Made Easy

Whether you're trying to get your diet on track, lose weight, or manage a variety of other health issues, the plant-based diet is a great place to start. The plant-based diet is a useful tool for weight management and weight loss, since it focuses on healthy whole foods instead of highly processed alternatives. But more than that, it's been associated with reducing the risk or symptoms of other diseases, like heart disease, diabetes, and cancer. You may even find some short-term health benefits, like increased energy, productivity, and ability to focus due to all the nutrients you're adding to your diet.

It might sound like a lot to expect of a few simple diet changes, but the results are definitely worth the effort. Fortunately, you can take a few easy steps to get started on the plant-based diet while still enjoying your favorite spicy dishes. If you're just starting out, consider choosing one or two small changes to focus on over a few weeks. Once you get comfortable with those, try adding in some of the more challenging ones. Here are some ideas to get you started:

- **Plan your meals in advance.** Planning your meals ahead of time can be a huge time-saver and can help you de-stress at the end of the day, since you already know exactly what you're going to eat. You can even try meal prepping and cooking ahead. You'll find that it's much easier to stick to a healthy, plant-based meal plan when all you need to do is heat up a dinner you've already made.
- **Be smart about grocery shopping.** The main focus of your grocery trip is going to be in the produce section...but don't feel bad about taking a detour to the frozen foods aisle to help stock up on your vegetables. Using frozen food can be a great way to cut down on your cook time on a busy night and to find favorite vegetables during the off-season.
- **Consider locating a farmers' market or produce co-op.** Both celebrate the "farm to table" mentality by offering locally grown foods. Local producers often offer a cost benefit too—a full bag of groceries may cost a fraction of the price at your neighborhood supermarket.
- **Avoid eating highly processed foods whenever you can.** That doesn't mean you have to always skip the occasional plate of cheesy jalapeño nachos on a Friday night with friends, but it does mean you should focus on achieving the right balance in your day-to-day meals. Do your best to choose whole foods that are complete as nature intended them, since highly processed foods are often stripped of their natural nutrients.
- **Rethink your snacks.** Consider making your own healthy snacks and bringing them with you when you're out and about during the day. You'll find these homemade snacks will be healthier than the pre-packaged processed alternatives while still giving you the energy you need. And because you can adjust the amount of spice you add, your midafternoon snack is completely customized to your perfect level of heat!
- **Find a support system.** That might mean looking for support online or with roommates, friends, and family members. Reach out to others who have an understanding of the diet who can share their experiences (and spiciest recipes!) with you.

The Plant-Based Diet Goes Spicy

Now that you know the basics of the plant-based diet, it's time to add some spice. Did you know that adding a little heat actually has health benefits beyond what you'll already be getting by going plant-based? Chili peppers contain large amounts of vitamins C and A, as well as healthy doses of vitamin E and potassium. They're also rich in antioxidants. It even doesn't matter what type of chili pepper you favor—the nutritional value is roughly the same in every pepper, regardless of the variety.

A Word of Caution

Despite the many benefits of enjoying spicy peppers, it's important to handle them carefully in the kitchen. You can't see or taste capsaicin (the substance that gives chili peppers all of their fire), but your mouth, eyes, nose, and skin certainly can. It's a serious irritant, and one that increases with a pepper's spiciness. For this reason, when handling chilies in the kitchen and prepping them for cooking, it's a good idea to put on a pair of rubber gloves. Be careful, of course, not to touch your eyes or nose or any other sensitive areas with your gloved hands.

If you prefer not to don gloves at all, be extremely cautious and remember to wash your hands thoroughly with soap and water after you are done handling the peppers. For those who intend to go gloveless, another idea is to handle the hot peppers under running water. By doing this, some of the capsaicin will immediately be washed away before it can seep into your skin and scald you.

There is less to worry about when handling dried chili peppers. Since most of the water has evaporated from the fruit, there's no risk of fresh juices squirting out onto skin or into eyes. However, capsaicin oils are still present, so be careful and, again, be sure to rinse your hands off after you are done handling the dried chilies.

And with that word of advice, it's time to start cooking! From delicious breakfasts like the Spicy Three-Pepper Frittata to main dishes like Easy Pad Thai Noodles and even sweet treats like Mexican Hot Chocolate, you'll find everything you need to bring the heat to your plant-based kitchen.

Chapter Two

RED-HOT BASICS (SAUCES, SPREADS, SALSAS, AND SPICES)

Carolina Barbecue Sauce

SERVES 6

This spicy sauce has a more acidic taste than the sweeter, mainstream, ketchup-based sauces.

Ingredients

4 tablespoons vegan margarine

1 cup apple cider vinegar

1/3 cup brown sugar

1 tablespoon molasses

1 tablespoon yellow mustard

2 teaspoons vegan Worcestershire sauce

1/8 teaspoon cayenne pepper

In a slow cooker, combine all ingredients. Cover and cook on high for 1 hour, stirring occasionally.

Per Serving

Calories: 99 | Fat: 3g | Sodium: 107mg
Carbohydrates: 16g | Fiber: 0g
Sugar: 15g | Protein: 0g

Coconut Curry Sauce

SERVES 6

Red curry paste is ideal for this recipe, but any variety will do.

Ingredients

1 (14-ounce) can coconut milk

1 cup Vegetable Broth
  (see recipe in Chapter 6)

1 teaspoon soy sauce

1 tablespoon curry paste

1 tablespoon freshly squeezed lime juice

2 medium cloves garlic, peeled
  and minced

$\frac{1}{2}$ teaspoon salt

$\frac{1}{4}$ cup chopped fresh cilantro

1. In a slow cooker, combine all ingredients except cilantro. Cover and cook on low for 2 hours.

2. Add cilantro and cook for an additional 30 minutes.

Per Serving

Calories: 136 | Fat: 13g | Sodium: 320mg
Carbohydrates: 3g | Fiber: 0g
Sugar: 0g | Protein: 2g

Easy Peanut Sauce

SERVES 6

Choose a peanut butter that is free of added flavors and is as natural as possible, so that it won't distort the flavors in your dish.

Ingredients

1 cup smooth peanut butter

$\frac{1}{4}$ cup maple syrup

$\frac{1}{2}$ cup sesame oil

1 teaspoon cayenne pepper

$1\frac{1}{2}$ teaspoons ground cumin

1 teaspoon garlic powder

$1\frac{1}{2}$ teaspoons salt

2 cups water

1. In a blender, add all ingredients except water. Add water slowly while blending until sauce reaches the desired consistency.

2. Pour sauce into a 2-quart slow cooker. Cover and cook on low for 1 hour.

Per Serving

Calories: 452 | Fat: 39g | Sodium: 583mg
Carbohydrates: 19g | Fiber: 4g
Sugar: 11g | Protein: 11g

USES FOR PEANUT SAUCE

Easy Peanut Sauce can be used to dress Asian noodles such as udon or soba noodles. You can also try it as a dipping sauce for steamed broccoli or spring rolls.

Easy Asian Dipping Sauce
YIELDS 1/3 CUP

Tangy, salty, spicy, and a bit sour—this easy dipping sauce has it all! Use it for dipping vegan sushi or as an excellent marinade for a baked tofu dish.

Ingredients

$1/4$ cup soy sauce

2 tablespoons rice vinegar

2 teaspoons sesame oil

1 teaspoon granulated sugar

1 teaspoon minced fresh ginger

2 medium cloves garlic, peeled and crushed

$1/4$ teaspoon red pepper flakes

In a small bowl, whisk together all ingredients until combined.

Per 1/3 Cup

Calories: 143 | Fat: 9g | Sodium: 3,503mg
Carbohydrates: 10g | Fiber: 1g
Sugar: 5g | Protein: 6g

Mole

SERVES 6

Just like barbecue sauce in the United States, Mexican mole sauce recipes vary greatly by region, and no two are exactly the same.

Ingredients

2 tablespoons olive oil

$\frac{1}{2}$ medium yellow onion, peeled and finely diced

3 medium cloves garlic, peeled and minced

1 teaspoon ground cumin

$\frac{1}{4}$ teaspoon ground cinnamon

$\frac{1}{4}$ teaspoon coriander

1 tablespoon chili powder

2 canned chipotle peppers in adobo sauce, drained and minced

1 teaspoon salt

4 cups Vegetable Broth (see recipe in Chapter 6)

1 ounce vegan dark chocolate, chopped

1. In a medium skillet over medium heat, add oil and sauté onion and garlic for 3 minutes. Add cumin, cinnamon, and coriander, and sauté for 1 minute.

2. Transfer sautéed mixture to a 4-quart slow cooker. Add chili powder, chipotles, and salt. Whisk in Vegetable Broth, then stir in chocolate.

3. Cover and cook on high for 2 hours.

Per Serving

Calories: 88 | Fat: 7g | Sodium: 492mg
Carbohydrates: 6g | Fiber: 2g
Sugar: 3g | Protein: 1g

Tempeh Mole
SERVES 4

Enjoy this flavorful plant-based Mexican sauce on top of a variety of proteins. Try serving this Tempeh Mole with a bed of brown rice or warm wheat tortillas.

Ingredients

2 tablespoons olive oil

1 medium yellow onion, peeled and chopped

4 medium cloves garlic, peeled and minced

2 tablespoons all-purpose wheat flour

2 teaspoons Better Than Bouillon No Chicken Base

3 cups water

2 tablespoons chili powder

1 teaspoon ground cumin

1 teaspoon dried oregano

1/2 teaspoon ground cinnamon

1/3 cup semisweet vegan chocolate chips

1/2 teaspoon salt

1/8 teaspoon black pepper

1 (12-ounce) package tempeh, cut into bite-sized squares

1. In a medium skillet over medium heat, add oil and sauté onion and garlic for 3 minutes. Add flour and whisk mixture to create a roux. Transfer to a 4-quart slow cooker.

2. Add all remaining ingredients. Cover and cook on high for 2 hours.

Per Serving

Calories: 379 | Fat: 22g | Sodium: 1,539mg
Carbohydrates: 28g | Fiber: 4g
Sugar: 10g | Protein: 19g

Tomatillo Sauce
SERVES 4

Tomatillos look like small green tomatoes. They are close relatives to the cape gooseberry (another name for ground cherry).

Ingredients

12 medium tomatillos, husked

Water, as needed

1 medium yellow onion, peeled and diced

2 medium cloves garlic, peeled and minced

1 medium jalapeño pepper, stemmed, seeded, and minced

$\frac{1}{2}$ tablespoon chopped fresh cilantro

1 teaspoon salt

1. In a slow cooker, add whole tomatillos with enough water to cover them. Cook on high for 1–2 hours or until tender. Drain tomatillos.

2. In a food processor, combine tomatillos, onion, garlic, jalapeño, cilantro, and salt. Process until puréed. Transfer mixture to a large bowl and add water until it has the consistency of a sauce.

Per Serving

Calories: 46 | Fat: 1g | Sodium: 583mg
Carbohydrates: 9g | Fiber: 3g
Sugar: 5g | Protein: 1g

Cranberry-Jalapeño Relish
SERVES 6

If you can't take the heat, leave the jalapeños out of this recipe for a more traditional relish.

Ingredients

1 (12-ounce) bag fresh or frozen cranberries

$\frac{1}{2}$ cup freshly squeezed orange juice

$\frac{1}{4}$ cup freshly squeezed lemon juice

1 cup granulated sugar

1 medium jalapeño pepper, stemmed, seeded, and minced

$\frac{1}{8}$ cup water

$\frac{1}{4}$ teaspoon salt

$\frac{1}{4}$ teaspoon black pepper

In a 4-quart slow cooker, combine all ingredients. Cover and cook on low for 2–3 hours.

Per Serving

Calories: 167 | Fat: 0g | Sodium: 98mg
Carbohydrates: 43g | Fiber: 3g
Sugar: 38g | Protein: 0g

Spicy Vegetable Marinara
SERVES 4

No Parmesan is needed to top off this hot and spicy vegetable marinara. Toss in a handful of TVP (textured vegetable protein) or browned, store-bought mock meat crumbles for a "meaty" sauce.

Ingredients

2 tablespoons olive oil

4 medium cloves garlic, peeled and minced

1 medium carrot, peeled and thinly sliced

2 medium stalks celery, trimmed and chopped

1 tablespoon plus ½ teaspoon red pepper flakes, divided

1 (28-ounce) can diced tomatoes, undrained

1 (6-ounce) can tomato paste

1 teaspoon dried oregano

1 teaspoon dried parsley

2 tablespoons chopped fresh basil

2 bay leaves

2 medium jalapeño peppers, stemmed, seeded, and diced

½ cup corn kernels

½ cup sliced black olives

1 tablespoon balsamic vinegar

½ teaspoon salt

1. In a large skillet over high heat, add oil and sauté garlic, carrot, celery, and 1 tablespoon red pepper flakes, stirring frequently until soft, about 4–5 minutes.

2. Reduce heat to low, then add tomatoes, tomato paste, oregano, parsley, basil, bay leaves, and jalapeños, stirring well to combine.

3. Cover and simmer for at least 30 minutes, stirring frequently.

4. Add corn, olives, vinegar, remaining red pepper flakes, and salt. Simmer uncovered for another 5 minutes.

5. Remove bay leaves before serving.

Per Serving

Calories: 208 | Fat: 10g | Sodium: 1,147mg
Carbohydrates: 26g | Fiber: 7g
Sugar: 13g | Protein: 5g

IN A PINCH
Don't have time to make marinara from scratch? Take 5 minutes to heat a store-bought variety on the stove and add in frozen veggies, Italian seasonings, and a bit of wine or balsamic vinegar for a fresh taste.

Simple Salsa

YIELDS 1 CUP

This simple, spicy condiment pairs magnificently with burritos, tacos, empanadas, tortilla chips, and all kinds of other Mexican savories.

Ingredients

2 large tomatoes, cored and quartered

1 small yellow onion, peeled and finely diced

2 medium jalapeño peppers, stemmed, seeded, and finely chopped

$\frac{1}{2}$ teaspoon freshly squeezed lime juice

$\frac{1}{8}$ teaspoon salt

$\frac{1}{8}$ teaspoon black pepper

$\frac{1}{2}$ teaspoon chipotle purée

1. Scrape seeds and pulp from tomato quarters; reserve. Chop tomato quarters into a fine dice. In a food processor, process reserved tomato seeds and pulp until smooth.

2. In a small bowl, stir together diced tomatoes, tomato pulp, onion, jalapeños, lime juice, salt, black pepper, and chipotle purée. This is best served the day it's made, but it can be refrigerated in an airtight container for up to 2 days.

Per 1 Cup

Calories: 101 | Fat: 1g | Sodium: 310mg
Carbohydrates: 23g | Fiber: 6g
Sugar: 14g | Protein: 4g

Rancheros Salsa

YIELDS 4 CUPS

This spicy salsa freezes exceptionally well. Consider making a double batch and storing half for later.

Ingredients

2 tablespoons olive oil

1 medium white onion, peeled and roughly chopped

1 medium red bell pepper, stemmed, seeded, and roughly chopped

1 medium green bell pepper, stemmed, seeded, and roughly chopped

4 medium plum tomatoes, cored and roughly chopped

1 tablespoon chopped garlic

1 (14-ounce) can diced tomatoes in tomato purée

1 (7-ounce) can crushed tomatillos, drained

1 (7-ounce) can green chilies, rinsed, drained, and roughly chopped

1 teaspoon chipotle purée

1 medium jalapeño pepper, stemmed, seeded, and finely chopped

$\frac{1}{4}$ cup chopped fresh cilantro

1 tablespoon frozen orange juice concentrate

1 teaspoon ground cumin, toasted in a dry pan until fragrant

1 teaspoon dried oregano

$\frac{1}{4}$ teaspoon ground cinnamon

$\frac{1}{8}$ teaspoon salt

$\frac{1}{8}$ teaspoon black pepper

1. In a large, heavy-bottomed pot, heat oil over medium-high heat until hot but not smoky. Add onion, bell peppers, and plum tomatoes, and sauté until onion is translucent, about 5 minutes.

2. In a food processor, combine garlic, diced tomatoes, and tomatillos, and process until puréed; add to onion mixture. Cook for 5 minutes more. Add green chilies, chipotle purée, jalapeño, and cilantro. Stir in orange juice concentrate, cumin, oregano, cinnamon, salt, and black pepper. Cook for 5 additional minutes before serving.

Per 1 Cup

Calories: 155 | Fat: 7g | Sodium: 425mg
Carbohydrates: 21g | Fiber: 6g
Sugar: 10g | Protein: 3g

Pressure Cooker Tomatillo Salsa
SERVES 8

Serve this Pressure Cooker Tomatillo Salsa with corn tortilla chips or as an accompaniment to Black Bean Dip (see recipe in Chapter 4).

Ingredients

1 pound tomatillos, husked, trimmed, and cut in half

2 medium jalapeño peppers, seeded and chopped

1/2 medium yellow onion, peeled and chopped

1/2 cup cold water

1/2 cup chopped fresh cilantro

2 teaspoons salt

1. In a pressure cooker, add tomatillos and enough water to cover. Lock the lid into place; bring to high pressure and maintain for 2 minutes. Remove from heat and allow pressure to release naturally.

2. Drain tomatillos. In a food processor or blender, combine tomatillos, jalapeños, onion, and 1/2 cup cold water. Process until well combined. Add cilantro and salt, and pulse until combined. Refrigerate salsa for about 4 hours before serving, to allow flavors to blend.

Per Serving

Calories: 21 | Fat: 0g | Sodium: 582mg
Carbohydrates: 4g | Fiber: 1g
Sugar: 3g | Protein: 1g

TOMATILLO
The tomatillo is a small yellowish or green fruit that grows on a vine in a paper husk. A relative of the ground cherry, tomatillos are a member of the nightshade family, as are tomatoes.

Pico de Gallo
YIELDS 2½ CUPS

This is a classic, fresh salsa that's easy to throw together just minutes before eating. This salsa tastes best in summer, when tomatoes are at their juiciest and most flavorful. For more spice, don't seed the jalapeños.

Ingredients

1 medium white onion, peeled and finely chopped

4 medium tomatoes, cored and finely chopped

3 medium jalapeño peppers, stemmed, seeded, and finely chopped

½ cup finely chopped fresh cilantro

1 tablespoon freshly squeezed lime juice

⅛ teaspoon salt

1. In a large bowl, combine all ingredients and mix thoroughly.

2. If there is time, let it sit in the refrigerator for 20 minutes to allow flavors to blend.

Per 1 Cup

Calories: 58 | Fat: 1g | Sodium: 128mg
Carbohydrates: 13g | Fiber: 4g
Sugar: 4g | Protein: 2g

PICO DE GALLO: WHAT'S IN A NAME?

Pico de gallo translates literally as "the beak of the rooster." The exact reason for the name is unknown, though perhaps it's because the tomatoes' red hue is reminiscent of the bird's beak. Pico de gallo is also beloved because it contains the three colors of the Mexican flag: red, white, and green.

Roasted Tomatillo Salsa

YIELDS ABOUT 2½ CUPS

This is a relatively simple salsa, but taking the time to roast the tomatillos, chilies, garlic, and scallions gives the salsa an extra smoky and charred flavor that is well worth the effort.

Ingredients

1 pound tomatillos, husked and trimmed

3 dried chilies de árbol

2 medium cloves garlic, peeled

3 medium scallions, trimmed

2 tablespoons chopped fresh cilantro

¼ teaspoon dried oregano

⅛ teaspoon salt

1. Using a comal or cast iron skillet set over medium-high heat, roast tomatillos, chilies, garlic, and scallions until tomatillos are softened and blackened, about 10 minutes.

2. In a blender, combine roasted vegetables with cilantro, oregano, and salt. Blend until smooth.

3. Store in an airtight container in the refrigerator, where it will keep for up to 2 weeks.

Per 1 Cup

Calories: 66 | Fat: 1g | Sodium: 120mg
Carbohydrates: 12g | Fiber: 4g
Sugar: 7g | Protein: 2g

WHAT IS A COMAL?

A comal is a smooth, flat griddle, usually cast iron, used throughout Mexico and Latin America to cook tortillas, toast spices, and roast chilies and vegetables. In many cultures, the comal is handed down from generation to generation, with the idea that the comal becomes better and more seasoned with age. If you don't have a comal, don't worry—a cast iron pan will do.

Mango-Citrus Salsa

YIELDS 2 CUPS

Salsa has a variety of uses, and this recipe adds color and variety to your usual chips and dip or Mexican dishes. Garnish with extra chopped cilantro and enjoy with tortilla chips.

Ingredients

1 medium mango, peeled, pitted, and chopped

2 medium tangerines, peeled and chopped

$1/2$ medium red bell pepper, stemmed, seeded, and chopped

$1/2$ medium red onion, peeled and minced

3 medium cloves garlic, peeled and minced

$1/2$ medium jalapeño pepper, stemmed, seeded, and minced

2 tablespoons freshly squeezed lime juice

$1/2$ teaspoon salt

$1/4$ teaspoon black pepper

3 tablespoons chopped fresh cilantro

1. In a large bowl, combine all ingredients. Gently toss to mix well.

2. Allow to sit for at least 15 minutes before serving to allow flavors to blend. Store any leftover salsa in an airtight container in the refrigerator.

Per 1 Cup

Calories: 178 | Fat: 1g | Sodium: 587mg
Carbohydrates: 45g | Fiber: 6g
Sugar: 35g | Protein: 3g

Mango-Habanero Salsa

YIELDS ABOUT 4 CUPS

This is a great salsa to enjoy in the summer. The juicy, sweet mangoes offer a nice contrast to the ultra-hot habanero pepper.

Ingredients

3 tablespoons canola oil

3 medium cloves garlic, unpeeled

3 medium tomatillos, husked and trimmed

3 medium tomatoes, cored

1 medium red bell pepper

1 medium yellow bell pepper

1 medium orange habanero chili pepper

1 medium red onion, peeled and finely chopped

1/4 cup chopped fresh cilantro

1/4 cup freshly squeezed lime juice

1 large mango, peeled, pitted, and cut into 1/4" cubes

1/8 teaspoon salt

1. Set an oven rack 6" from the top heating unit and pre-heat oven broiler to high. Line a baking sheet with foil.

2. In a large bowl, combine oil, garlic, tomatillos, tomatoes, bell peppers, and habanero. Toss to coat vegetables with oil.

3. Transfer vegetables to prepared baking sheet and set under the broiler. Broil vegetables, turning a few times, until they are charred and blistered, about 10 minutes.

4. Transfer garlic, tomatillos, and tomatoes to a large bowl; let cool. Return bell peppers and habanero to the oven and continue broiling until soft, 3–5 minutes longer. Remove from oven and let them steam in a separate covered bowl for a few minutes.

5. In a blender or food processor, add tomatillos and tomatoes. Peel garlic and add to blender. Peel blackened skin from bell peppers and habanero, remove stems and seeds, and add peppers to blender. Blend all vegetables until finely chopped.

6. In a large bowl, combine blended vegetables with red onion, cilantro, lime juice, and mango. Season with salt. Store any leftover salsa in an airtight container in the refrigerator.

Per 1 Cup

Calories: 211 | Fat: 11g | Sodium: 82mg
Carbohydrates: 28g | Fiber: 5g
Sugar: 18g | Protein: 3g

Chili de Árbol Salsa
YIELDS 2 CUPS

Chilies de árbol are a staple in many salsas because of their strong heat and naturally subtle, smoky flavor. This salsa puts those flavors at the forefront.

Ingredients

½ pound Roma tomatoes

½ pound tomatillos, husked and trimmed

1 cup chilies de árbol

½ bunch fresh cilantro, leaves only, roughly chopped

1 medium white onion, peeled and chopped

4 medium cloves garlic, peeled and lightly smashed

2 cups water

1 teaspoon salt

1. Set an oven rack 6" from the top heating unit and preheat oven broiler to high. Line a baking sheet with foil.

2. Spread tomatoes and tomatillos on prepared baking sheet and set under the broiler. Broil, turning occasionally, until vegetables are charred, 10–12 minutes.

3. In a large saucepan over medium-high heat, combine tomatoes and tomatillos with remaining ingredients. Bring mixture to a boil and cook until onion is soft, about 12 minutes.

4. Transfer sauce to a blender or food processor. Blend until smooth, then strain into a bowl.

5. Store leftover salsa in the refrigerator, where it will keep for about 1 week.

Per 1 Cup

Calories: 110 | Fat: 1g | Sodium: 1,179mg
Carbohydrates: 23g | Fiber: 5g
Sugar: 13g | Protein: 4g

Pineapple Salsa

YIELDS 2 CUPS

This is another great tropical salsa that's especially nice in the summer. If you can, let it sit for 30 minutes before serving to give all the flavors time to blend.

Ingredients

2 cups diced fresh pineapple

½ cup chopped fresh cilantro

¼ cup finely chopped red onion

1 medium serrano chili pepper, stemmed, seeded, and finely chopped

Juice and zest of 1 medium lime

¼ teaspoon salt

1. In a large bowl, combine all ingredients and toss to mix well.

2. Store any leftover salsa in an airtight container in the refrigerator.

Per 1 Cup

Calories: 93 | Fat: 0g | Sodium: 294mg
Carbohydrates: 25g | Fiber: 3g
Sugar: 17g | Protein: 1g

Raw Tomatillo Salsa
YIELDS 1½ CUPS

This simple salsa, called cruda, is probably the easiest way to make a salsa from tomatillos. This sauce may seem a bit thin at first, but it will thicken as it stands.

Ingredients

1 pound tomatillos, husked and trimmed

4 medium serrano chili peppers, stemmed, seeded, and roughly chopped

1 cup roughly chopped fresh cilantro

1 large clove garlic, peeled and roughly chopped

⅛ teaspoon salt

1. In a small saucepan over medium heat, add tomatillos with just enough water to cover, and bring to a simmer. Simmer until softened, about 10 minutes. Drain, reserving ½ cup of the cooking water.

2. In a blender, combine reserved cooking water, serranos, cilantro, and garlic. Blend until almost smooth.

3. Add cooked tomatillos in small batches, blending briefly after each addition. The sauce should be chunky and rough.

4. Transfer to a bowl and stir in salt. Store any leftover salsa in an airtight container in the refrigerator.

Per 1 Cup

Calories: 100 | Fat: 2g | Sodium: 202mg
Carbohydrates: 19g | Fiber: 6g
Sugar: 12g | Protein: 3g

Smoky Chipotle Salsa
YIELDS ABOUT 2 CUPS

Chipotles add a surprise smoky flavor to this salsa, which also has plenty of sweetness from roasted tomatoes. Serve this as a table salsa with chips for a delicious snack.

Ingredients

8 medium tomatoes, cored

1 medium yellow onion, peeled and halved

4 dried chipotle chili peppers

2 medium cloves garlic, peeled

$1/8$ teaspoon salt

$1/2$ cup water

1. Using a comal or cast iron skillet set over medium heat, roast tomatoes, onion, chipotles, and garlic until nearly blackened, about 10 minutes.

2. In a blender, combine roasted vegetables and salt and add water. Blend until smooth, adding more water if needed to achieve desired consistency.

Per 1 Cup

Calories: 160 | Fat: 1g | Sodium: 172mg
Carbohydrates: 33g | Fiber: 7g
Sugar: 19g | Protein: 5g

Peanut Salsa

YIELDS 2 CUPS

This unusual salsa originated on the Gulf Coast of Mexico. Spread this hot sauce on top of warm wheat tortillas, or serve over brown rice.

Ingredients

1 cup shelled roasted unsalted peanuts

2 cups water, divided

4 canned chipotle peppers in adobo sauce, drained and roughly chopped

2 medium cloves garlic, peeled and roughly chopped

2 black peppercorns

2 whole cloves

2 tablespoons vegetable oil

$\frac{1}{8}$ teaspoon salt

1. In a coffee grinder or food processor, grind peanuts until they are a fine powder.

2. In a blender, combine $\frac{1}{2}$ cup water, chipotles, garlic, peppercorns, and cloves. Blend well.

3. In a small skillet over medium heat, add oil and blended ingredients. Sauté for 4 minutes, stirring constantly to avoid sticking. Gradually stir in ground peanuts and cook for another 2 minutes.

4. Add remaining water and salt and continue cooking, stirring and scraping the bottom of the pan, for another 5 minutes. Remove from heat and serve.

Per 1 Cup

Calories: 581 | Fat: 45g | Sodium: 532mg
Carbohydrates: 23g | Fiber: 10g
Sugar: 6g | Protein: 18g

Avocado Salsa

YIELDS 4 CUPS

This is a tangy green salsa made smooth and silky by the addition of avocados. You can use it on tacos or in enchiladas, but you just might find yourself eating it straight with a spoon. Be sure to use soft, ripe avocados. Garnish with chopped cilantro and enjoy with your favorite fresh vegetable dippers.

Ingredients

6 medium tomatillos, husked and coarsely chopped

2 medium jalapeño peppers, stemmed, seeded, and coarsely chopped

3 medium cloves garlic, peeled

2 tablespoons water

3 medium avocados, peeled, pitted, and thinly sliced

5 sprigs fresh cilantro

1 teaspoon salt

1½ cups vegan sour cream

1. In a medium saucepan over medium-high heat, combine tomatillos, jalapeños, garlic, and water. Bring to a boil, then reduce heat and simmer for 10 minutes. Remove from heat and let cool a bit.

2. In a food processor or blender, combine the cooked vegetables with avocados, cilantro, and salt. Blend until smooth. Add a little water if necessary to loosen mixture from blender blades.

3. Pour into a bowl and stir in sour cream.

Per 1 Cup

Calories: 341 | Fat: 29g | Sodium: 665mg
Carbohydrates: 22g | Fiber: 14g
Sugar: 3g | Protein: 3g

Creamy Pumpkin Seed and Habanero Salsa
YIELDS 1½ CUPS

This salsa, called sikil pak, is a traditional Mayan recipe from the Yucatan Peninsula. It's incredibly creamy, yet there is no trace of dairy. Be careful when handling the roasted habanero here—consider gloves!

Ingredients

3 medium tomatoes, cored

½ large white onion, peeled and thickly sliced

1 habanero chili pepper

1 cup shelled pumpkin seeds, toasted

½ cup fresh cilantro leaves

⅛ teaspoon salt

1. Using a comal or cast iron skillet set over medium heat, roast tomatoes, onion, and habanero until softened and a little black, about 5 minutes over medium-high heat. Carefully seed and roughly chop habanero.

2. In a food processor or blender, combine roasted vegetables with pumpkin seeds, cilantro, and salt. Pulse until well blended. The salsa should be thick and creamy. Add a little water to thin if necessary.

Per 1 Cup

Calories: 122 | Fat: 1g | Sodium: 220mg
Carbohydrates: 30g | Fiber: 9g
Sugar: 16g | Protein: 6g

Mixed Chili Salsa

YIELDS 1½ CUPS

This raw salsa is bright and colorful. If you are lucky enough to live near a market that sells a variety of chilies, be sure to make this. Feel free to vary it with whatever chilies are fresh and available.

Ingredients

1 medium poblano chili pepper, stemmed, seeded, and finely chopped

1 medium red jalapeño pepper, stemmed, seeded, and finely chopped

2 medium yellow chili peppers (such as a güero or Anaheim), stemmed, seeded, and finely chopped

2 medium serrano chili peppers, seeds intact, finely chopped

½ medium white onion, peeled and finely chopped

2 medium tomatoes, cored, seeded, and finely chopped

3 tablespoons freshly squeezed lime juice

½ teaspoon dried oregano

⅛ teaspoon salt

1. In a large nonreactive bowl, combine all ingredients and mix well.

2. Let sit for 1 hour in the refrigerator before serving to allow flavors to blend.

Per 1 Cup

Calories: 94 | Fat: 1g | Sodium: 206mg
Carbohydrates: 22g | Fiber: 6g
Sugar: 7g | Protein: 4g

GÜERO

Güero chilies are medium-hot peppers that are a yellow color. They are also sometimes called gold spike chilies. *Güero* translates from Spanish to "blond," though it is also called out on the streets in Mexico as a generic nickname (not necessarily derogatively) for light-haired or light-skinned tourists and locals.

Roasted Corn Salsa

YIELDS 3½ CUPS

This is a great spicy salsa to make in summer, when corn on the cob is bursting with sweetness. You can serve with chips or put it on tacos, but it's also hearty enough to be a side dish.

Ingredients

Kernels from 3 medium ears corn

2 tablespoons unsalted vegan margarine

4 medium scallions, trimmed and thinly sliced, white and green parts separated

2 medium cloves garlic, peeled and minced

1½ teaspoons salt, divided

1½ teaspoons ground cumin, divided

1 teaspoon chili powder, divided

½ teaspoon black pepper

2 medium plum tomatoes, stemmed, seeded, and finely diced

2 medium jalapeño peppers, trimmed (seeds retained) and finely diced

1. Heat a dry, large, cast iron skillet over medium-high heat and pan-roast corn kernels, stirring occasionally until golden brown, about 8–9 minutes. Transfer to a bowl.

2. Add margarine to skillet along with white parts of scallions, garlic, 1 teaspoon salt, ½ teaspoon cumin, ½ teaspoon chili powder, and black pepper. Cook until scallions are tender, about 3 minutes.

3. Remove pan from heat and stir in corn, tomatoes, jalapeños, green parts of scallions, and remaining salt, cumin, and chili powder.

4. Serve warm, or refrigerate before serving.

Per 1 Cup

Calories: 104 | Fat: 4g | Sodium: 1,036mg
Carbohydrates: 21g | Fiber: 3g
Sugar: 7.2g | Protein: 4g

Guajillo Salsa

YIELDS 3 CUPS

This is a salsa of medium heat, with plenty of nice chili flavor from the guajillos. You can serve it as a table salsa or heat it with 2 tablespoons chili oil to make a hot sauce.

Ingredients

½ pound dried guajillo chili peppers, stemmed

3 cups hot water

5 large cloves garlic, peeled and roasted until soft

1 teaspoon ground cumin

1 teaspoon salt

½ pound Roma tomatoes, cored

2 teaspoons shelled pumpkin seeds, toasted

⅓ cup apple cider vinegar

1 teaspoon dried oregano

1. Using a comal or cast iron skillet set over medium heat, lightly toast guajillos, about 3 minutes.

2. Transfer guajillos to a small bowl and cover with hot water. Let them sit until softened, at least 15 minutes.

3. Drain guajillos, reserving water. Chop guajillos roughly.

4. In a blender or food processor, combine guajillos with remaining ingredients. Blend until the mixture forms a paste. Add a little chili water to thin if necessary.

Per 1 Cup

Calories: 308 | Fat: 1g | Sodium: 808mg
Carbohydrates: 49g | Fiber: 1g
Sugar: 2g | Protein: 12g

PUMPKIN SEEDS

Called *pepitas* in Spanish, pumpkin seeds are commonly used in Mexican cuisine as a thickener for sauces. Along with adding body to salsas and moles, pumpkin seeds add a warm, nutty flavor to dishes.

Super-Spicy Salsa
YIELDS 3½ CUPS

You can use this hot and spicy salsa in so many ways. It's wonderful in frittatas and delicious as a garnish for chili.

Ingredients

2 medium jalapeño peppers, stemmed, seeded, and minced

1 medium habanero chili pepper, stemmed, seeded, and minced

1 medium green bell pepper, stemmed, seeded, and minced

4 medium cloves garlic, peeled and minced

1 medium red onion, peeled and chopped

5 medium tomatoes, cored and chopped

3 tablespoons freshly squeezed lemon juice

¼ teaspoon salt

⅛ teaspoon white pepper

¼ cup chopped fresh cilantro

1. In a large bowl, combine jalapeños, habanero, bell pepper, garlic, onion, and tomatoes.

2. In a small bowl, combine lemon juice, salt, and white pepper; stir to dissolve salt. Add to tomato mixture along with cilantro.

3. Cover and refrigerate for 3–4 hours before serving.

Per 1 Cup

Calories: 230 | Fat: 1g | Sodium: 625mg
Carbohydrates: 53g | Fiber: 13g
Sugar: 29g | Protein: 10g

Zesty Black Bean Salsa
SERVES 10

This hearty, filling, spicy salsa gets its body from fiber-rich black beans.

Ingredients

1 cup chopped red onion

¼ cup chopped fresh cilantro

¼ cup chopped fresh parsley

1 medium jalapeño pepper, seeded

1½ cups cooked black beans

4 cups chopped tomatoes

3 tablespoons freshly squeezed lime juice

2 tablespoons olive oil

⅛ teaspoon black pepper

1. In a food processor, combine onion, cilantro, parsley, and jalapeño; finely chop.

2. In a medium bowl, combine onion mixture, beans, and tomatoes.

3. In a separate small bowl, whisk together lime juice, olive oil, and black pepper. Pour over beans; mix well. Chill before serving.

Per Serving

Calories: 79 | Fat: 3g | Sodium: 5mg
Carbohydrates: 11g | Fiber: 4g
Sugar: 3g | Protein: 3g

USING CANNED BEANS VERSUS COOKING YOUR OWN

Canned beans are very convenient and can save you time. Keep in mind that the sodium content of recipes will be higher with canned beans. Reduce sodium content in canned beans by draining and thoroughly rinsing with cold water before using.

Homemade Chili Powder

YIELDS ½ CUP

Of course you can go to any store and buy chili powder in a bottle, but where's the fun in that? Making your own is easy and, best of all, you can customize it however you like. Here's a basic recipe, but feel free to tinker with it and add more heat or use different types of chilies.

Ingredients

4 dried ancho chili peppers, stemmed, seeded, and roughly chopped

4–5 dried chilies de árbol, stemmed and seeded

2 tablespoons ground cumin

2 tablespoons garlic powder

1 tablespoon dried oregano

1 teaspoon paprika

½ teaspoon cayenne pepper

1. Using a comal or cast iron skillet set over medium-high heat, lightly toast anchos and chilies de árbol until they puff slightly, about 5 minutes.

2. In a food processor or blender, combine toasted chilies and blend until they form a fine powder. Transfer to a small bowl.

3. Add remaining ingredients and stir well until thoroughly mixed.

4. Store in an airtight container in a cool, dry place for up to 6 months.

Per ½ Cup

Calories: 339 | Fat: 7g | Sodium: 71mg
Carbohydrates: 58g | Fiber: 24g
Sugar: 1g | Protein: 14g

ORIGINS OF CHILI POWDER

No one knows the exact origins of chili powder, but the original version of what you see in supermarkets was created in the United States sometime in the nineteenth century. Chili powder was developed as the way to flavor the southwestern staple chili con carne. For every household that made chili, there was likely a unique chili powder blend.

Berbere

SERVES 8

This complex, heady spice mix is the foundation for all Ethiopian cooking. There are a lot of ingredients, but it's well worth all the grinding and mixing. Try to use whole spices as much as possible, and feel free to adjust seasoning to your liking.

Ingredients

1 teaspoon fenugreek seeds

½ cup dried red chilies

½ cup hot paprika

2 tablespoons salt

1 teaspoon ground ginger

2 teaspoons onion powder

1 teaspoon ground green cardamom

1 teaspoon ground nutmeg

1 teaspoon garlic powder

¼ teaspoon ground cloves

½ teaspoon ground cinnamon

¼ teaspoon ground allspice

1. Grind seeds and chilies in a spice or coffee grinder. Be careful not to inhale all the bits of spice that will be released during the process.

2. In a medium bowl, add ground spices with remaining ingredients. Stir well until completely combined.

3. Store in an airtight container in the refrigerator for up to 3 months.

Per Serving

Calories: 34 | Fat: 1g | Sodium: 1,750mg
Carbohydrates: 7g | Fiber: 3g
Sugar: 1g | Protein: 2g

BERBERE

In Ethiopia, the process of making berbere can take days—even up to a week. Chilies are often dried in the sun for multiple days, then ground by hand with a mortar and pestle. Then the chilies are combined with other spices and left to dry in the sun again. While the fundamental flavors are the same, families each have their own unique berbere recipe and mix.

Creole Seasoning Blend
YIELDS ABOUT 1 CUP

The building block for so many great southern dishes like gumbo and jambalaya, this spice blend also works great as a rub for barbecued veggies.

Ingredients

5 tablespoons hot paprika

3 tablespoons salt

2 tablespoons garlic powder

2 tablespoons onion powder

2 tablespoons dried oregano

2 tablespoons dried basil

2 tablespoons black pepper

1 tablespoon dried thyme

1 tablespoon cayenne pepper

1 tablespoon white pepper

1. In a small bowl, combine all ingredients and stir well.

2. Store in an airtight container in a cool, dry place for up to 6 months.

Per 1 Cup

Calories: 308 | Fat: 6g | Sodium: 20,981mg
Carbohydrates: 68g | Fiber: 38g
Sugar: 6g | Protein: 14g

Adobo Seasoning

YIELDS 1½ CUPS

Adobo is a spice mixture that is used throughout Latin America and the Caribbean. Try it on veggies—then grill, roast, or fry.

Ingredients

6 tablespoons salt

6 tablespoons granulated garlic

2 tablespoons black pepper

2 tablespoons onion powder

2 tablespoons ground cumin

2 tablespoons coriander

2 tablespoons chili powder (a smoky chipotle chili powder would be good, but use whatever you have on hand)

¼ teaspoon allspice

½ teaspoon dried oregano

1. In a small bowl, add all ingredients and stir until thoroughly combined.

2. Store in an airtight container in a cool, dry place for up to 1 year.

Per 1 Cup

Calories: 262 | Fat: 4g | Sodium: 28,256mg
Carbohydrates: 54g | Fiber: 15g
Sugar: 2g | Protein: 12g

Curry Powder
YIELDS 1 CUP

This basic Curry Powder recipe, which you should customize to your own liking, will give you a new appreciation for this complex spice mix that adds flavor to so many dishes. Use ground spices or grind your own.

Ingredients

6 tablespoons coriander

4 tablespoons ground cumin

2 tablespoons black pepper

2 tablespoons ground cinnamon

1 tablespoon turmeric

1 tablespoon ground ginger

1 tablespoon cayenne pepper

1 teaspoon ground nutmeg

1 teaspoon ground cloves

1. In a small bowl, add all ingredients and stir until well combined.

2. Store in an airtight container in a cool, dry place for up to 6 months.

Per 1 Cup

Calories: 300 | Fat: 8g | Sodium: 94mg
Carbohydrates: 52g | Fiber: 28g
Sugar: 2g | Protein: 11g

TURMERIC

Turmeric is the spice that gives all curry powder its distinct yellow-orange hue. Turmeric has an astringent yet earthy flavor, akin to mustard or horseradish, but more mellow. Its strong color will dye any food that it is sprinkled on. You might also find fresh turmeric at specialty grocery stores, where it looks similar to its cousin ginger.

Ras El Hanout
YIELDS ¼ CUP

The Arabic phrase *ras el hanout* means "top of the shop" and refers to a spice owner's special blend of his best spices. It's an essential Moroccan spice mix, and some versions have upward of twenty or even thirty ingredients.

Ingredients

1 teaspoon ground cloves

1 teaspoon ground ginger

1 teaspoon ground cardamom

1 teaspoon ground mace

1 teaspoon ground nutmeg

1 teaspoon black pepper

1 teaspoon ground cinnamon

1 teaspoon ground allspice

1 teaspoon turmeric

1 teaspoon hot paprika

1. In a small bowl, combine all the spices and stir until thoroughly mixed.

2. Store in an airtight container in a cool, dry place for up to 6 months.

Per ¼ Cup

Calories: 66 | Fat: 2g | Sodium: 8mg
Carbohydrates: 14g | Fiber: 6g
Sugar: 1g | Protein: 2g

Baharat

YIELDS ½ CUP

Baharat is a spice mix used throughout the Middle East, including in Lebanon, Syria, Israel, and Jordan. Its name simply means "spice" in Arabic. There are endless variations, so feel free to experiment. Try Baharat on different vegetables.

Ingredients

2 tablespoons black pepper

2 tablespoons hot paprika

1 tablespoon coriander

1 tablespoon ground cumin

1 tablespoon ground cloves

1 tablespoon dried mint

2 teaspoons ground nutmeg

1 teaspoon ground cinnamon

1. In a small bowl, combine all ingredients and stir to mix well.

2. Store in an airtight container in a cool, dry place for up to 6 months.

Per ½ Cup

Calories: 157 | Fat: 5g | Sodium: 52mg
Carbohydrates: 29g | Fiber: 16g
Sugar: 2g | Protein: 6g

Chapter Three

BREAKFAST AND BRUNCH

Tofu Frittata

SERVES 4

Frittatas are traditionally made with eggs, but you can use tofu instead for a plant-based breakfast dish that is guaranteed to spice up brunch!

Ingredients

2 tablespoons olive oil

1 cup peeled and diced red potatoes

1/2 medium yellow onion, peeled and diced

1/2 cup diced red bell pepper

1/2 cup diced green bell pepper

1 teaspoon minced jalapeño pepper

1 medium clove garlic, peeled and minced

1/4 cup chopped fresh parsley

1 (16-ounce) package firm tofu, drained

1/2 cup unsweetened soy milk

4 teaspoons cornstarch

2 tablespoons nutritional yeast

1 teaspoon yellow mustard

1/2 teaspoon turmeric

1 teaspoon salt

1/4 teaspoon black pepper

1. In a large skillet over medium heat, add oil and sauté potatoes, onion, bell peppers, jalapeño, and garlic until softened, about 15–20 minutes.

2. Meanwhile, in a blender or food processor, combine remaining ingredients and blend until smooth. Pour mixture into a 4-quart slow cooker; add potato mixture.

3. Cover and cook on high for 4 hours, or until frittata has firmed.

Per Serving

Calories: 213 | Fat: 11g | Sodium: 636mg
Carbohydrates: 16g | Fiber: 3g
Sugar: 4g | Protein: 13g

Hot and Spicy Home Fries
SERVES 6

Home fries are traditionally made in a pan or skillet on the stovetop, but they can be easily adapted for the slow cooker.

Ingredients

2 pounds red potatoes, peeled and chopped

1 medium yellow onion, peeled and chopped

1 medium green bell pepper, stemmed, seeded, and chopped

2 tablespoons olive oil

$\frac{1}{2}$ teaspoon ground cumin

2 teaspoons paprika

1 teaspoon chili powder

1 teaspoon salt

$\frac{1}{4}$ teaspoon black pepper

In a 4-quart slow cooker, combine all ingredients. Cover and cook on high for 2 hours.

Per Serving

Calories: 111 | Fat: 5g | Sodium: 405mg
Carbohydrates: 17g | Fiber: 2g
Sugar: 3g | Protein: 2g

Potato-Poblano Breakfast Burritos
SERVES 2

This hot and spicy breakfast is sure to fill you up! Add your favorite vegan cheese if desired. Garnish with chopped cilantro if you like.

Ingredients

2 tablespoons olive oil

2 small russet potatoes, diced small

2 medium poblano chili peppers, stemmed, seeded, and diced

1 teaspoon chili powder

1/8 teaspoon salt

1/8 teaspoon black pepper

1 medium tomato, cored and diced

2 (10") wheat tortillas, warmed

1 teaspoon hot sauce

1. In a large skillet over medium-high heat, add oil and sauté potatoes and poblanos until potatoes are almost soft, about 6–7 minutes.

2. Add chili powder, salt, black pepper, and tomato, and stir well to combine.

3. Continue cooking until potatoes and tomatoes are soft, another 4–5 minutes.

4. To serve, wrap in warmed wheat tortillas and drizzle with hot sauce.

Per Serving

Calories: 472 | Fat: 17g | Sodium: 420mg
Carbohydrates: 77g | Fiber: 14g
Sugar: 6g | Protein: 13g

Chili Masala Tofu Scramble
SERVES 2

Tofu scramble is an easy and versatile vegan breakfast. This version adds chili and curry to pump up the flavor. Toss in whatever veggies you have on hand—tomatoes, spinach, or diced broccoli would work well.

Ingredients

1 (16-ounce) package firm or extra-firm tofu, drained

2 tablespoons olive oil

1 small yellow onion, peeled and diced

2 medium cloves garlic, peeled and minced

1 small red chili pepper, minced

1 medium green bell pepper, stemmed, seeded, and chopped

3/4 cup sliced button mushrooms

1 tablespoon soy sauce

1 teaspoon curry powder

1/2 teaspoon ground cumin

1/4 teaspoon turmeric

1 teaspoon nutritional yeast

1. To press tofu, wrap drained tofu block in a clean kitchen towel. Place on a plate and weigh it down with a stack of plates or a heavy skillet. Allow to drain for 15 minutes.

2. Cut or crumble pressed tofu into 1" cubes.

3. In a large skillet over medium-high heat, add oil and sauté onion and garlic until soft, about 5 minutes.

4. Add tofu, chili pepper, bell pepper, and mushrooms, stirring well to combine.

5. Add remaining ingredients except yeast, and combine well. Allow to cook until tofu is lightly browned, about 6–8 minutes.

6. Remove from heat and stir in yeast.

Per Serving

Calories: 334 | Fat: 22g | Sodium: 474mg
Carbohydrates: 15g | Fiber: 5g
Sugar: 6g | Protein: 22g

THE NEXT DAY
Leftover tofu scramble makes an excellent lunch, or wrap leftovers in a warmed wheat tortilla to make breakfast-style burritos. Why isn't it called "scrambled tofu" instead of "tofu scramble" if it's a substitute for scrambled eggs? This is one of the great conundrums of veganism.

Tofu Ranchero

SERVES 4

Bring Mexican cuisine to the breakfast table with this easy Tofu Ranchero cooked in your slow cooker.

Ingredients

3 tablespoons olive oil

1 (16-ounce) package firm tofu, drained and crumbled

1/2 medium yellow onion, peeled and diced

2 medium cloves garlic, peeled and minced

Juice of 1 medium lemon

1/2 teaspoon turmeric

1 teaspoon salt

1/4 teaspoon black pepper

1 cup cooked pinto beans, drained and rinsed

8 (10") wheat tortillas

1/2 cup (2 ounces) shredded vegan Cheddar cheese

1/2 cup chipotle salsa

1. In a 4-quart slow cooker, combine oil, tofu, onion, garlic, lemon juice, turmeric, salt, pepper, and pinto beans. Cover and cook on high for 4 hours.

2. Preheat the oven to 350°F.

3. When ranchero filling is nearly done, in a small skillet over medium-high heat, brown tortillas on both sides.

4. Place tortillas on a baking sheet and divide filling equally among them. Sprinkle cheese over filling, leave open-faced, and bake until cheese has melted, about 5 minutes. Top with chipotle salsa.

Per Serving

Calories: 668 | Fat: 28g | Sodium: 1,240mg
Carbohydrates: 91g | Fiber: 17g
Sugar: 10g | Protein: 27g

Jalapeño Hash Browns

SERVES 6

The type of jalapeños you choose for this plant-based dish can make the heat vary greatly, so add what you like!

Ingredients

2 tablespoons olive oil

2 pounds red potatoes, peeled and shredded

1 medium yellow onion, peeled and diced

¼ cup chopped pickled jalapeño peppers

1 teaspoon salt

¼ teaspoon black pepper

In a 4-quart slow cooker, combine all ingredients. Cover and cook on high for 2 hours.

Per Serving

Calories: 161 | Fat: 4g | Sodium: 452mg
Carbohydrates: 28g | Fiber: 2g
Sugar: 3g | Protein: 3g

Onion, Pepper, and Poblano Hash

SERVES 4

Use a cheese grater to achieve finely grated potatoes for this spicy dish.

Ingredients

2 tablespoons olive oil

4 cups peeled and grated russet potatoes

½ medium yellow onion, peeled and diced

1 medium poblano chili pepper, stemmed, seeded, and diced

2 medium cloves garlic, peeled and minced

1 teaspoon chili powder

½ teaspoon paprika

½ teaspoon ground cumin

1 teaspoon salt

¼ teaspoon black pepper

In a 4-quart slow cooker, combine all ingredients. Cover and cook on high for 4 hours.

Per Serving

Calories: 217 | Fat: 7g | Sodium: 611mg
Carbohydrates: 36g | Fiber: 4g
Sugar: 2g | Protein: 4g

BETTER HASH BROWNS

After you have grated the potatoes for the hash browns, make sure to rinse them in a colander to get rid of the extra starch. Then allow the potatoes to dry so they will get extra crispy in the slow cooker.

Spicy Three-Pepper Frittata

SERVES 4

Frittatas are traditionally made with eggs, but you can use tofu to make this easy pressure cooker Spicy Three-Pepper Frittata plant-based instead. Garnish with extra chopped peppers if you'd like.

Ingredients

2 tablespoons olive oil

1 cup peeled and diced red potatoes

½ cup diced white or yellow onion

½ cup diced red bell pepper

½ cup diced green bell pepper

1 teaspoon minced jalapeño pepper

1 medium clove garlic, peeled and minced

¼ cup chopped fresh parsley

1 (16-ounce) package firm tofu, drained

½ cup unsweetened soy milk

4 teaspoons cornstarch

2 teaspoons nutritional yeast

1 teaspoon yellow mustard

½ teaspoon turmeric

1 teaspoon salt

1. Preheat the oven to 400°F. Lightly spray a 9" quiche pan or pie plate with nonstick cooking spray.

2. In a pressure cooker on low heat, add oil, potatoes, onion, bell peppers, jalapeño, garlic, and parsley, and sauté for 3 minutes. Lock the lid in place and bring to high pressure; maintain pressure for 6 minutes. Remove from heat and quick-release the pressure.

3. In a blender or food processor, combine tofu, soy milk, cornstarch, yeast, mustard, turmeric, and salt. Blend until smooth, then add to cooked potato mixture.

4. Spoon mixture into prepared quiche pan. Bake for 45 minutes, or until frittata is firm, then remove from heat and let stand for 10 minutes before serving.

Per Serving

Calories: 213 | Fat: 11g | Sodium: 629mg
Carbohydrates: 17g | Fiber: 3g
Sugar: 4g | Protein: 12g

MAKE IT A SCRAMBLE

To shorten the preparation time for this meal while keeping all of the flavors, try making this plant-based dish into a scramble by preparing the entire recipe in the pressure cooker. Skip the step of blending the tofu and omit the cornstarch. Add remaining ingredients, breaking apart tofu as you stir, and sauté until cooked through.

Spicy Breakfast Burrito

SERVES 4

Tofu is a great alternative to eggs in breakfast dishes, and it is naturally plant-based!

Ingredients

2 tablespoons olive oil

1 (16-ounce) package firm tofu, drained and crumbled

$\frac{1}{4}$ cup diced red onion

1 tablespoon minced jalapeño pepper

$\frac{1}{4}$ cup diced red bell pepper

$\frac{1}{4}$ cup diced poblano chili pepper

1 cup cooked black beans, drained and rinsed

2 teaspoons turmeric

1 teaspoon ground cumin

$\frac{1}{2}$ teaspoon chili powder

$\frac{1}{2}$ teaspoon salt

$\frac{1}{4}$ teaspoon black pepper

4 (10") wheat tortillas

1 medium avocado, peeled, pitted, and sliced

$\frac{1}{2}$ cup diced tomatoes

$\frac{1}{4}$ cup chopped fresh cilantro

$\frac{1}{2}$ cup chipotle salsa

1. In a large skillet on high heat, add oil and sauté tofu, onion, jalapeño, bell pepper, and poblano until soft, about 5–8 minutes.

2. Transfer to a 4-quart slow cooker on high. Add black beans, turmeric, cumin, chili powder, salt, and black pepper. Reduce heat to low, cover, and cook for 4 hours.

3. Divide filling evenly among tortillas, and top each with avocado, tomatoes, cilantro, and salsa. Fold the sides of tortillas in and roll up the burritos.

Per Serving

Calories: 475 | Fat: 21g | Sodium: 690mg
Carbohydrates: 57g | Fiber: 15g
Sugar: 7g | Protein: 22g

STEAMING TORTILLAS

To warm and soften tortillas, for best results, steam tortillas on the stovetop using a steamer basket over a saucepan of boiling water for 3 minutes. If you're in a hurry, throw the tortillas into the microwave one at a time and heat for about 30 seconds on high.

Red Pepper Grits

SERVES 6

Grits are a true southern staple, but this recipe has a slight twist and calls for Vegetable Broth and red pepper flakes.

Ingredients

2 cups stone-ground grits

3 cups water

3 cups Vegetable Broth
(see recipe in Chapter 6)

2 tablespoons vegan margarine

2 teaspoons red pepper flakes

1 teaspoon salt

$\frac{1}{4}$ teaspoon black pepper

In a 4-quart slow cooker, combine all ingredients. Cover and cook on high for 2 hours.

Per Serving

Calories: 211 | Fat: 2g | Sodium: 417mg
Carbohydrates: 42g | Fiber: 1g
Sugar: 1g | Protein: 5g

CHOOSING GRITS
You may be most familiar with instant or fast-cooking grits, but those should be avoided in slow cooker recipes. Choose stone-ground or whole-kernel grits instead; they will hold up better during the long cooking time.

Foul

SERVES 4

Foul (pronounced "FOOL") is a classic Egyptian breakfast. A far cry from sugary sweet cereal, it's spicy and satisfying and tastes best when scooped with pieces of warm pita or crusty French bread.

Ingredients

½ cup plus 2 tablespoons olive oil, divided

2 medium cloves garlic, peeled and finely chopped

1 small yellow onion, peeled and finely chopped

1 large tomato, seeded and roughly chopped, divided

½ teaspoon chili powder

½ teaspoon ground cumin

1 (19-ounce) can fava beans, liquid reserved

1 small cucumber, peeled, seeded, and finely chopped

2 medium jalapeño peppers, stemmed, seeded, and finely chopped

2 tablespoons fresh parsley, finely chopped

2 tablespoons fresh mint leaves, finely chopped

2 tablespoons freshly squeezed lemon juice

1. In a medium saucepan over medium-high heat, add 2 tablespoons oil and sauté garlic, onion, half the tomato, chili powder, and cumin until soft and fragrant, about 5 minutes.

2. Add fava beans with their liquid. Bring to a boil, then reduce heat to low and let simmer until tender, about 10–15 minutes. Remove from heat and let cool. Drain, but reserve cooking liquid.

3. In a large bowl, combine bean mixture with cucumber, jalapeños, parsley, mint, lemon juice, and remaining oil. Toss to combine. If you like a little more sauce, add a little of the reserved cooking liquid.

Per Serving

Calories: 423 | Fat: 33g | Sodium: 358mg
Carbohydrates: 24g | Fiber: 7g
Sugar: 4g | Protein: 8g

FAVA BEANS

Fava beans are native to North Africa and used extensively in North African and Middle Eastern cooking. They are a key ingredient in Egyptian falafel, soups, and stews. If you can't find fava beans at the store, you can substitute canned or dried brown beans.

Sunrise Tofu Scramble
SERVES 4

Go gourmet with this spicy tofu scramble by substituting shiitake mushrooms and Japanese eggplant for the broccoli and button mushrooms.

Ingredients

1 (16-ounce) package firm tofu, drained and crumbled

$\frac{1}{2}$ cup chopped broccoli florets

$\frac{1}{2}$ cup sliced button mushrooms

2 tablespoons olive oil

2 teaspoons turmeric

1 teaspoon ground cumin

$\frac{1}{4}$ teaspoon garlic powder

$\frac{1}{2}$ teaspoon red pepper flakes

2 medium cloves garlic, peeled and minced

1 teaspoon salt

$\frac{1}{4}$ teaspoon black pepper

$\frac{1}{2}$ cup diced tomato

$\frac{1}{4}$ cup freshly squeezed lemon juice

2 tablespoons chopped fresh parsley

1. In a 4-quart slow cooker, combine tofu, broccoli, mushrooms, oil, turmeric, cumin, garlic powder, red pepper flakes, minced garlic, salt, and black pepper. Cover and cook on low for 4 hours.

2. Add tomato, lemon juice, and parsley.

Per Serving

Calories: 164 | Fat: 11g | Sodium: 606mg
Carbohydrates: 7g | Fiber: 3g
Sugar: 2g | Protein: 11g

Poblano Hash Browns
SERVES 4

Any type of pepper will do, such as poblano, jalapeño, or bell pepper, in these spicy, pressure cooker Poblano Hash Browns.

Ingredients

4 cups peeled and grated russet potatoes

2 tablespoons olive oil

2 tablespoons vegan margarine

¼ cup diced white or yellow onion

1 medium poblano chili pepper, stemmed, seeded, and diced

1 medium clove garlic, peeled and minced

⅛ teaspoon salt

⅛ teaspoon black pepper

1 teaspoon ground cumin

1. Rinse grated potatoes in a colander, then allow to air-dry or squeeze dry by wrapping in a clean kitchen towel. Set aside.

2. In a pressure cooker over high heat, add oil and margarine and sauté onion and poblano until just soft, about 5 minutes.

3. Add garlic and potatoes; sauté for an additional 5 minutes, stirring occasionally, until potatoes are just beginning to brown. Season with salt, black pepper, and cumin.

4. Use a wide metal spatula to press the potatoes down firmly in the cooker.

5. Lock the lid in place and bring to low pressure; maintain pressure for 6 minutes. Remove from heat and quick-release the pressure.

Per Serving

Calories: 215 | Fat: 9g | Sodium: 122mg
Carbohydrates: 30g | Fiber: 3g
Sugar: 3g | Protein: 3g

Chapter Four

APPETIZERS AND SNACKS

Black Bean Dip

SERVES 12

To give this dip an extra kick, you can substitute canned jalapeño peppers for the mild green chilies or add 2 teaspoons chipotle chili powder.

Ingredients

1 cup dried black beans

2 cups water

1 tablespoon olive oil

1 small yellow onion, peeled and diced

3 medium cloves garlic, peeled and minced

1 (14.5-ounce) can diced tomatoes, undrained

2 (4-ounce) cans finely chopped mild green chilies, undrained

1 teaspoon chili powder

1/2 teaspoon dried oregano

1/4 cup finely chopped fresh cilantro

1/8 teaspoon salt

1 cup shredded Monterey jack cheese

1. In a medium bowl or pot, combine beans and water. Cover and let beans soak for 8 hours at room temperature.

2. In a pressure cooker, add oil and sauté onion until soft, about 5 minutes. Add garlic and sauté for 30 seconds.

3. Drain beans and add to pressure cooker along with tomatoes, green chilies, chili powder, and oregano. Stir well. Lock the lid into place. Bring to high pressure; maintain pressure for 12 minutes. Remove from heat and allow pressure to release naturally for 10 minutes.

4. Quick-release any remaining pressure. Remove lid.

5. In a food processor or blender, combine cooked beans mixture with cilantro and salt, and process until smooth.

6. Transfer the dip to a medium serving bowl and stir in cheese. Serve warm.

Per Serving

Calories: 119 | Fat: 4g | Sodium: 213mg
Carbohydrates: 14g | Fiber: 5g
Sugar: 2g | Protein: 7g

OTHER BEAN OPTIONS

Bean dips are delicious when made with a variety of dried beans. To complement the flavors in this recipe, use black beans, pinto beans, or white beans. If you're pressed for time, use canned beans instead of dried beans, but be sure to drain the liquid first.

Curry Dip
YIELDS 2 1/2 CUPS

Serve this spicy dip with toasted bread or your favorite crackers!

Ingredients

1 teaspoon olive oil

1/2 cup finely chopped onion

1/2 medium jalapeño pepper, stemmed, seeded, and finely chopped

2 teaspoons finely chopped red bell pepper

1 teaspoon curry powder

1 teaspoon ground cumin

1/2 teaspoon coriander

1/2 teaspoon turmeric

1/4 teaspoon cayenne pepper

1/2 teaspoon salt

1 tablespoon raisins, softened overnight in 1/2 cup water, drained

1 1/2 cups vegan mayonnaise

1 tablespoon chopped fresh cilantro

1/4 teaspoon freshly squeezed lemon juice

1. In a small skillet over medium heat, add oil and sauté onion, jalapeño, and bell pepper until soft, about 5 minutes. Add curry powder, cumin, coriander, turmeric, cayenne pepper, and salt. Cook 1 minute more, until spices are very fragrant. Add raisins and about 1 tablespoon water. Remove from heat.

2. Transfer to a food processor. Process on high speed for 30 seconds; scrape down sides of bowl with a rubber spatula. Add mayonnaise, cilantro, and lemon juice; process 30 seconds more, until smooth and even.

Per 1 Cup

Calories: 916 | Fat: 88g | Sodium: 1,286mg
Carbohydrates: 9g | Fiber: 2g
Sugar: 4g | Protein: 1g

Seitan Buffalo Wings
SERVES 4

To tame these spicy "wings," dip in a cooling dairy-free ranch dressing or serve with chilled cucumber slices.

Ingredients

2 cups vegetable oil

⅓ cup vegan margarine

⅓ cup Louisiana Hot Sauce

1 cup flour

1 teaspoon garlic powder

1 teaspoon onion powder

¼ teaspoon cayenne pepper

½ cup unsweetened soy milk

1 (16-ounce) package traditional seitan, chopped

1. In a deep-fat fryer or large pot over medium heat, heat oil to 350°F.

2. In a large skillet over low heat, combine the margarine and Louisiana Hot Sauce just until margarine is melted. Set aside.

3. In a small bowl, combine the flour, garlic powder, onion powder, and cayenne pepper. Place soy milk in a separate bowl.

4. Dip each piece of seitan in the soy milk, then dredge in flour mixture. Carefully place in hot oil and deep-fry until lightly golden brown on all sides, about 4–5 minutes.

5. Coat fried seitan with margarine and hot sauce mixture.

Per Serving

Calories: 374 | Fat: 20g | Sodium: 1,251mg
Carbohydrates: 23g | Fiber: 2g
Sugar: 2g | Protein: 22g

BAKED, NOT FRIED

This is, admittedly, not the healthiest of vegan recipes, but you can cut some of the fat out by skipping the breading and deep-frying. Instead, lightly brown the seitan in a bit of oil, then coat with the sauce. Alternatively, bake the seitan with the sauce for 25 minutes at 325°F.

Texas Caviar

YIELDS 5 CUPS

Prepare this pressure cooker dip up to 2 days in advance and store in a covered container in the refrigerator.

Ingredients

1 cup dried black-eyed peas

8 cups water, divided

$\frac{1}{4}$ cup red wine vinegar

2 tablespoons olive oil

1 teaspoon salt

$\frac{1}{2}$ teaspoon black pepper

$\frac{1}{2}$ teaspoon ground cumin

1 pound cooked corn kernels

$\frac{1}{2}$ medium yellow onion, peeled and diced

$\frac{1}{2}$ medium green bell pepper, stemmed, seeded, and diced

1 medium pickled jalapeño pepper, finely chopped

1 medium tomato, cored and diced

2 tablespoons chopped fresh cilantro

1. In a small bowl, combine black-eyed peas with 4 cups of water; soak for 1 hour. Drain and rinse.

2. In a pressure cooker, combine drained black-eyed peas with remaining water. Lock the lid into place; bring to high pressure and maintain for 11 minutes. Remove from heat and allow pressure to release naturally. Drain.

3. In a large bowl, whisk together vinegar, oil, salt, black pepper, and cumin until well combined. Add drained black-eyed peas and remaining ingredients. Toss to combine. Refrigerate 1–2 hours before serving to allow flavors time to blend.

Per 1 Cup

Calories: 248 | Fat: 7g | Sodium: 509mg
Carbohydrates: 42g | Fiber: 8g
Sugar: 9g | Protein: 7g

Eggplant Baba Ghanoush

YIELDS 1¹/₂ CUPS

Whip up a batch of this Eggplant Baba Ghanoush and some Roasted Red Pepper Hummus (see recipe in this chapter) to make a spicy Mediterranean appetizer spread. Don't forget some vegan pita bread to dip into your dish.

Ingredients

2 medium eggplants, trimmed and sliced in half lengthwise

3 tablespoons olive oil, divided

2 tablespoons freshly squeezed lemon juice

¼ cup tahini

3 medium cloves garlic, peeled and minced

½ teaspoon ground cumin

½ teaspoon chili powder

¼ teaspoon salt

1 tablespoon chopped fresh parsley

1. Preheat oven to 400°F. Prick eggplants several times with a fork.

2. Place on a baking sheet and drizzle with 1 tablespoon olive oil. Bake for 30 minutes, or until soft. Allow to cool slightly.

3. Scoop out inner flesh and place in a large bowl.

4. Using a large fork or potato masher, mash eggplant together with remaining ingredients until almost smooth.

Per 1 Cup

Calories: 638 | Fat: 46g | Sodium: 456mg
Carbohydrates: 51g | Fiber: 22g
Sugar: 22g | Protein: 14g

Spicy Soy Buffalo Strips

SERVES 6

Most bottled buffalo wing sauces contain butter, so be sure to read the label or make your own by following the steps below.

Ingredients

$\frac{1}{3}$ cup vegan margarine

$\frac{1}{3}$ cup hot sauce

1 tablespoon apple cider vinegar

1 teaspoon garlic powder

$1\frac{1}{2}$ (10-ounce) packages Gardein Meatless Chick'n Strips

1. In a small microwave-safe bowl, microwave margarine on high for 30 seconds, or until melted.

2. Add hot sauce, vinegar, and garlic powder, and stir well.

3. In a 4-quart slow cooker, combine prepared hot sauce mixture and Chick'n Strips; stir to coat completely. Cook on low for 1 hour.

Per Serving

Calories: 147 | Fat: 9g | Sodium: 697mg
Carbohydrates: 4g | Fiber: 0g
Sugar: 0g | Protein: 11g

SERVING STRIPS

Faux buffalo chicken strips can be added to sandwiches or salads, but if you'd like to serve them as an appetizer or snack, place in a small basket lined with parchment paper and add sides of celery sticks, carrot sticks, and vegan ranch dressing.

Caramelized Onion and Mushroom Cheeseless Quesadillas

SERVES 6

Sure, you can easily make vegan quesadillas using vegan cheese, but try this more nutritious version filled with a "cheesy" bean spread. Garnish with extra jalapeño slices and chopped cilantro if you like.

Ingredients

2 tablespoons olive oil

½ medium yellow onion, peeled and chopped

1 cup sliced button mushrooms

½ cup chopped canned jalapeño slices

2 medium cloves garlic, peeled and minced

⅛ teaspoon salt

⅛ teaspoon black pepper

1 (15-ounce) can white beans (any variety), drained

1 medium tomato, cored

3 tablespoons nutritional yeast

3 tablespoons freshly squeezed lemon juice

½ teaspoon ground cumin

6 (10") wheat tortillas

1 tablespoon vegetable oil

1. In a large skillet over medium-high heat, add olive oil and sauté onion, mushrooms, jalapeños, and garlic. Sprinkle with salt and black pepper. Cook, stirring occasionally, until onion and mushrooms are browned and caramelized, about 8 minutes.

2. In a food processor or blender, combine white beans, tomato, yeast, lemon juice, and cumin. Process until smooth.

3. For each quesadilla, spread one-third of the bean mixture on a tortilla, then top with a portion of the mushrooms and onion. Top with a second tortilla.

4. In a large skillet over medium-high heat, add vegetable oil and lightly fry quesadillas for 2–3 minutes on each side, just until tortillas are lightly crispy.

Per Serving

Calories: 357 | Fat: 12g | Sodium: 476mg
Carbohydrates: 55g | Fiber: 10g
Sugar: 5g | Protein: 14g

Southwest Sweet Potato Enchiladas
SERVES 4

These hot and spicy enchiladas freeze well, so make a double batch and thaw and reheat when you're hungry!

Ingredients

2 medium sweet potatoes, baked, peeled, and diced

½ medium yellow onion, peeled and minced

3 medium cloves garlic, peeled and minced

1 (15-ounce) can black beans, drained and rinsed

2 teaspoons freshly squeezed lime juice

2 tablespoons sliced green chilies

2 teaspoons chili powder

1 teaspoon ground cumin

1 (15-ounce) can green chili enchilada sauce

½ cup water

12 (8") wheat tortillas, warmed

1. Preheat oven to 350°F.

2. In a large bowl, combine sweet potatoes, onion, garlic, beans, lime juice, chilies, chili powder, and cumin until well mixed.

3. In a separate small bowl, combine enchilada sauce with water. Add ¼ cup of this mixture to beans and sweet potatoes, and combine well.

4. Spread about ⅓ cup enchilada sauce in the bottom of a casserole or baking dish.

5. Place about ⅓ cup bean mixture in a tortilla and roll up. Place seam-side down in casserole dish. Repeat until all filling is used.

6. Spread a generous layer of remaining enchilada sauce over the top of the rolled tortillas, being sure to coat all the edges and corners well.

7. Bake for 25–30 minutes, until browned.

Per Serving

Calories: 597 | Fat: 9g | Sodium: 1,207mg
Carbohydrates: 112g | Fiber: 19g
Sugar: 16g | Protein: 20g

SWEET POTATO BURRITOS

Sweet potatoes and black beans make lovely vegan burritos as well as enchiladas. Omit the enchilada sauce and wrap the mixture in wheat tortillas along with the usual taco fixings.

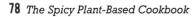

Garlic Confit
YIELDS 5 HEADS GARLIC

Use this confit in place of fresh garlic in recipes where you want a little spice, or enjoy it smashed and spread on toasted bread.

Ingredients

2 cups olive oil, or more as needed

5 heads garlic, cloves separated and peeled

3 medium dried red chili peppers

1. In a 4-quart slow cooker, combine all ingredients. Add more oil if necessary to cover all the garlic cloves. Cover and cook on low for 4 hours, or until garlic is tender.

2. Remove garlic with a slotted spoon and place in canning jars. Pour oil over garlic and seal the top.

Per 1 Head Garlic

Calories: 120 | Fat: 9g | Sodium: 5mg
Carbohydrates: 10g | Fiber: 1g
Sugar: 0g | Protein: 2g

PRESERVING GARLIC
Garlic confit is a great and easy way to preserve garlic when it is in season and at its peak. Garlic prepared using this method can be stored in an airtight container for up to 3 months in the refrigerator.

Jalapeño "Cheese" Dip

SERVES 12

To pump up the spice in this pressure cooker recipe, just add extra pickled jalapeños!

Ingredients

2 tablespoons vegan margarine

2 tablespoons all-purpose flour

1 cup unsweetened soy milk

4 cups (16 ounces) shredded vegan Cheddar cheese

½ cup canned diced tomatoes, undrained

½ cup pickled jalapeño peppers

2 tablespoons freshly squeezed lemon juice

⅛ teaspoon salt

⅛ teaspoon black pepper

1. In a pressure cooker, soften margarine over low heat and gradually stir in flour to form a roux. Add soy milk and stir until mixture has thickened and there are no lumps. Bring mixture to a boil.

2. Add cheese and stir until smooth. Add tomatoes and jalapeños, and secure the lid on the pressure cooker. Cook on high until the pressure indicator rises. Lower heat and cook for 3 minutes. Allow the pressure to release and remove the lid. Add lemon juice, salt, and black pepper.

Per Serving

Calories: 130 | Fat: 10g | Sodium: 484mg
Carbohydrates: 10g | Fiber: 2g
Sugar: 1g | Protein: 1g

Portobello and Pepper Fajitas
SERVES 4

Chopped seitan could take the place of the portobellos in these spicy fajitas if you prefer, or look for plant-based "steak" or "chicken" strips. Try topping them with salsa, sliced avocados, and vegan sour cream.

Ingredients

2 tablespoons olive oil

2 large portobello mushrooms, trimmed and cut into strips

1 medium green bell pepper, stemmed, seeded, and cut into strips

1 medium red bell pepper, stemmed, seeded, and cut into strips

1 medium yellow onion, peeled and cut into strips

$3/4$ teaspoon chili powder

$1/4$ teaspoon ground cumin

1 teaspoon hot sauce

1 tablespoon chopped fresh cilantro

4 (10") wheat tortillas, warmed

1. In a large skillet over medium-high heat, add oil and sauté mushrooms, bell peppers, and onion until vegetables are almost done, about 5 minutes.

2. Add chili powder, cumin, and hot sauce, and stir to combine. Cook until mushrooms and peppers are soft, 2–3 more minutes. Remove from heat and stir in fresh cilantro.

3. Divide vegetable mixture evenly among tortillas.

Per Serving

Calories: 287 | Fat: 12g | Sodium: 200mg
Carbohydrates: 43g | Fiber: 7g
Sugar: 7g | Protein: 9g

Nacho "Cheese" Dip
YIELDS ABOUT 1 CUP

Peanut butter in cheese sauce? Absolutely! Just a touch of peanut butter gives a creamy and nutty layer of flavor to this spicy sauce, and helps it to thicken nicely. Use this sauce to dress plain steamed veggies or make homemade nachos.

Ingredients

3 tablespoons vegan margarine

1 cup unsweetened soy milk

3/4 teaspoon garlic powder

1/2 teaspoon onion powder

1/2 teaspoon salt

1 tablespoon peanut butter

1/4 cup all-purpose flour

1/4 cup nutritional yeast

3/4 cup salsa

2 tablespoons chopped canned jalapeño peppers, drained

1. In a medium saucepan over low heat, combine margarine and soy milk. Add garlic powder, onion powder, and salt, stirring to combine. Add peanut butter and stir until melted.

2. Whisk in flour, 1 tablespoon at a time, until smooth. Heat until thickened, about 5–6 minutes.

3. Stir in yeast, salsa, and jalapeño peppers.

4. Allow to cool slightly before serving, as sauce will thicken as it cools.

Per 1 Cup

Calories: 567 | Fat: 23g | Sodium: 3,105mg
Carbohydrates: 56g | Fiber: 13g
Sugar: 19g | Protein: 23g

CHILI CHEESE
Add a can of store-bought vegan chili for a chili cheese dip, or smother some French fries to make chili cheese fries.

Chili "Cheese" Dip

SERVES 12

The perfect accompaniment for this spicy, slow cooker plant-based dip is salty corn tortilla chips.

Ingredients

1 (15-ounce) can vegetarian chili

¼ cup diced white or yellow onion

½ cup diced tomatoes

1 (8-ounce) package vegan cream cheese

1 cup (8 ounces) shredded vegan Cheddar cheese

1 teaspoon garlic powder

In a 4-quart slow cooker, combine all ingredients. Cover and heat on low for 1 hour.

Per Serving

Calories: 114 | Fat: 8g | Sodium: 347mg
Carbohydrates: 11g | Fiber: 2g
Sugar: 1g | Protein: 2g

PLANT-BASED CHILI
Most major grocery stores sell canned vegetarian chili. One of the easiest to find is Hormel Vegetarian Chili with Beans, which contains textured vegetable protein instead of meat.

Sinless Chili Cheese Fries

SERVES 4

Chili cheese fries sin carne (without meat) are almost healthy enough to eat as an entrée. Almost. But go ahead and eat them for dinner—you deserve it, and no one will ever know. Garnish with chopped parsley if you like.

Ingredients

1 (20-ounce) bag frozen French fries

1 tablespoon vegetable oil

1/2 medium yellow onion, peeled and chopped

1 (15-ounce) can kidney beans, drained and rinsed

1 1/2 cups TVP, rehydrated in water

1 1/3 cups tomato paste

2 tablespoons chili powder

1/2 teaspoon ground cumin

1/2 teaspoon cayenne pepper

2 tablespoons vegan margarine

2 tablespoons whole-wheat flour

1 1/2 cups unsweetened soy milk

2 tablespoons yellow mustard

1/2 teaspoon garlic powder

1/2 teaspoon salt

1/2 cup (2 ounces) grated vegan Cheddar cheese

1. Prepare French fries according to package instructions.

2. In a large skillet over medium-high heat, add oil and sauté onion until soft, about 5 minutes. Reduce heat to low and add beans, TVP, tomato paste, chili powder, cumin, and cayenne pepper. Cover and simmer until beans are tender, about 8–10 minutes.

3. In a separate medium saucepan over medium heat, melt margarine and flour together until thick and pasty, then stir in soy milk, mustard, garlic, and salt. Add cheese and heat just until melted and mixture has thickened.

4. Smother French fries with TVP chili, and top with cheese sauce.

Per Serving

Calories: 615 | Fat: 16g | Sodium: 1,904mg
Carbohydrates: 82g | Fiber: 20g
Sugar: 19g | Protein: 35g

Guacamole

SERVES 8

Serve this flavorful dip with tortilla chips or as an accompaniment to spicy food.

Ingredients

2 medium cloves garlic, peeled and chopped

$\frac{1}{4}$ cup chopped red onion

1 small jalapeño pepper, stemmed, seeded, and finely chopped

4 medium avocados, halved, pitted, and peeled

2 tablespoons freshly squeezed lime juice

$\frac{1}{2}$ teaspoon salt

$\frac{1}{8}$ teaspoon black pepper

$\frac{1}{4}$ cup chopped fresh cilantro

1 medium plum tomato, stemmed, seeded, and chopped

With a mortar and pestle, or in a medium bowl with a fork, mash together garlic, onion, and jalapeño. Add avocado and mash until it forms a chunky paste. Add lime juice, salt, black pepper, and cilantro, and stir to combine. Garnish with chopped tomato.

Per Serving

Calories: 121 | Fat: 9g | Sodium: 153mg
Carbohydrates: 8g | Fiber: 5g
Sugar: 1g | Protein: 2g

Frijole Dip
SERVES 12

For best results, serve this spicy slow cooker dip immediately after cooking or reheat if it cools. Keep in mind that if you make it the night before serving, the spices will have time to mingle, which results in a spicier dish!

Ingredients

2 (15-ounce) cans pinto beans, drained and rinsed

1½ cups water

1 tablespoon olive oil

1 small yellow onion, peeled and diced

3 medium cloves garlic, peeled and minced

1 cup diced tomatoes

1 teaspoon chipotle chili powder

½ teaspoon ground cumin

¼ cup finely chopped fresh cilantro

⅛ teaspoon salt

1 cup (4 ounces) shredded vegan Monterey jack cheese

1. In a 4-quart slow cooker, combine beans, water, oil, onion, and garlic. Cover and cook on low for 1 hour.

2. Mash the beans in the cooker until about half are smooth and half are still chunky.

3. Add all remaining ingredients. Stir well, cover, and cook for an additional 30 minutes.

Per Serving

Calories: 103 | Fat: 4g | Sodium: 227mg
Carbohydrates: 14g | Fiber: 1g
Sugar: 1g | Protein: 4g

Tofu and Portobello Enchiladas
SERVES 4

Turn up the heat by adding some fresh minced or canned chilies. If you're addicted to vegan cheese, add a handful of grated cheese to the filling as well as on top.

Ingredients

2 tablespoons oil

1 (16-ounce) package firm tofu, drained and diced small

5 medium portobello mushrooms, trimmed and chopped

1 medium yellow onion, peeled and diced

3 medium cloves garlic, peeled and minced

2 teaspoons chili powder

1/2 cup sliced black olives

1 (15-ounce) can enchilada sauce, divided

8 (10") wheat tortillas

1/2 cup vegan Cheddar cheese

1. Preheat oven to 350°F.

2. In a large skillet over medium-high heat, add oil and sauté tofu, mushrooms, onion, and garlic until tofu is just lightly sautéed, about 4–5 minutes. Add chili powder and heat for 1 more minute, stirring to coat well.

3. Remove from heat. Add olives and 1/3 cup enchilada sauce, and combine well.

4. Spread a thin layer of enchilada sauce in the bottom of a baking pan or casserole dish.

5. For each enchilada, place about 1/4 cup of the tofu and mushrooms on a tortilla and roll up. Place seam-side down in baking dish, fitting enchiladas together snugly. Top with remaining enchilada sauce, coating the tops of each tortilla well.

6. Sprinkle with cheese and bake for 25–30 minutes.

Per Serving

Calories: 668 | Fat: 28g | Sodium: 1,528mg
Carbohydrates: 91g | Fiber: 16g
Sugar: 17g | Protein: 28g

VEGETABLE ENCHILADAS
Omit the mushrooms and grate a couple of carrots and zucchini to use in the filling instead. They'll bake quickly when grated, so there's no need to precook them.

Vegetable Gado-Gado
SERVES 8

This appetizer of vegetables with a spicy peanut sauce is Indonesian in origin. Serve with assorted blanched vegetables.

Ingredients

$1/2$ cup smooth peanut butter

$1/4$ cup honey

$1/4$ teaspoon salt

$1/8$ teaspoon cayenne pepper

1 tablespoon freshly squeezed lime juice

$3/4$ cup canned coconut milk

In a food processor or large bowl, combine peanut butter, honey, salt, cayenne pepper, and lime juice; pulse or whisk together until smooth. Gradually work in coconut milk until a saucy consistency is reached. Adjust consistency further, if desired, with hot water.

Per Serving

Calories: 169 | Fat: 12g | Sodium: 75mg
Carbohydrates: 13g | Fiber: 2g
Sugar: 10g | Protein: 4g

Roasted Red Pepper Hummus
YIELDS 1½ CUPS

You'll rarely meet a plant-based foodie who doesn't love hummus in one form or another. As a veggie dip or sandwich spread, this spicy hummus is always a favorite. Up the cayenne pepper in this recipe if that's your thing, and don't be ashamed to lick the spoon.

Ingredients

1 (15-ounce) can chickpeas, drained

⅓ cup tahini

⅔ cup chopped bottled roasted red peppers

3 tablespoons freshly squeezed lemon juice

2 tablespoons olive oil

2 medium cloves garlic, peeled

½ teaspoon ground cumin

⅓ teaspoon salt

¼ teaspoon cayenne pepper

In a blender or food processor, combine all ingredients and process until smooth, scraping the sides down as needed.

Per 1 Cup

Calories: 734 | Fat: 45g | Sodium: 1,438mg
Carbohydrates: 62g | Fiber: 16g
Sugar: 12g | Protein: 22g

DO-IT-YOURSELF ROASTED RED PEPPERS

Sure, you can buy them in a jar, but it's easy to roast your own red peppers. Here's how: Fire up your oven to 450°F (or use the broiler setting) and drizzle a few whole peppers with olive oil. Bake for 30 minutes, turning over once. Direct heat will also work if you have a gas stove. Hold the peppers with tongs over the flame until lightly charred. Let your peppers cool, then remove the skin before making hummus.

Pintos, Cerveza, and Lime Dip

SERVES 6

If you don't have a Mexican cerveza on hand when making this spicy dip, a domestic beer will work just fine.

Ingredients

2 tablespoons olive oil

1/2 medium yellow onion, peeled and diced

3 medium cloves garlic, peeled and minced

1/2 pound dried pinto beans

3 cups plus additional water for processing

12 ounces Mexican beer

1 medium jalapeño pepper, stemmed, seeded, and minced

4 tablespoons freshly squeezed lime juice

1/4 teaspoon salt

1/8 teaspoon black pepper

1. In a medium skillet over high heat, add oil and sauté onion and garlic for 3–4 minutes.

2. Transfer to a slow cooker over high heat. Add beans, 3 cups water, and beer. Cover and cook on high until beans are tender, about 4–5 hours. Drain beans.

3. In a food processor, combine cooked beans, jalapeño, lime juice, salt, and black pepper. Process, adding enough water to achieve a smooth consistency. Serve hot or at room temperature.

Per Serving

Calories: 170 | Fat: 5g | Sodium: 98mg
Carbohydrates: 25g | Fiber: 8g
Sugar: 1g | Protein: 8g

Curried Mixed Nuts (Masala Nuts)

YIELDS 3 CUPS

Try variations of this using your favorite nuts, and spice them as you like.
Wooden chopsticks make great tools to stir the nuts.

Ingredients

1 teaspoon cumin seeds

1 teaspoon coriander seeds

1/4 teaspoon black peppercorns

2 whole cloves

1 medium dried red chili,
   roughly pounded

3 tablespoons vegetable oil

1/4 teaspoon ground ginger

3 cups unsalted raw mixed nuts

1 teaspoon salt

1. In a small skillet over medium heat, combine cumin seeds, coriander seeds, peppercorns, cloves, and dried chili. Toast the spices, stirring constantly, for about 3–5 minutes. They will darken and release a wonderful aroma. Remove from heat and transfer them to a bowl to cool. Using a spice grinder or a coffee grinder, grind the spices.

2. In a large skillet over low heat, add oil and sauté ground spice mixture, ginger, and nuts. Cook gently, stirring constantly, for about 3 minutes. Cover and cook for an additional 5 minutes, shaking the pan occasionally.

3. Remove from heat and sprinkle with salt. Cool to room temperature, then serve.

Per 1 Cup

Calories: 946 | Fat: 81g | Sodium: 796mg
Carbohydrates: 37g | Fiber: 13g
Sugar: 0g | Protein: 24g

SCORCHING SPICES

Sometimes adding powdered spices to an already hot pan can scorch them. If this is a problem for you, try adding 1 tablespoon water to the spices before you sauté them. The water will quickly evaporate and the spices will sauté without burning.

Spiced Pecans

YIELDS 3 CUPS

These pecans are great if you like a little spice in your life.

Ingredients

2 tablespoons vegan margarine

1 pound shelled whole pecans

2 tablespoons light soy sauce

1 tablespoon hoisin sauce

A few drops hot pepper sauce

1. Preheat oven to 325°F.

2. In a large skillet over medium heat, melt margarine. Add pecans and cook, tossing occasionally, until nuts are well coated, about 2 minutes. Add soy sauce, hoisin sauce, and hot pepper sauce; cook for 1 more minute. Stir to coat thoroughly.

3. Spread pecans in a single layer on a baking sheet. Bake for 20 minutes, until all liquid is absorbed and pecans begin to brown. Remove from oven. Cool before serving.

Per 1 Cup

Calories: 1,093 | Fat: 107g | Sodium: 728mg
Carbohydrates: 24g | Fiber: 15g
Sugar: 8g | Protein: 15g

Potato Pakoras (Fritters)

SERVES 8

Serve these feisty fritters immediately with chutney for dipping.

Ingredients

1¼ cups sifted chickpea flour

2 teaspoons vegetable oil

1½ teaspoons ground cumin

½ teaspoon cayenne pepper

¼ teaspoon turmeric

2½ teaspoons salt

½ cup cold water

1 (8-ounce) baking potato, peeled and sliced into ⅛" pieces

3 cups vegetable oil

1. In a food processor or blender, combine flour, oil, cumin, cayenne pepper, turmeric, and salt. Pulse three or four times until fluffy. With blade spinning, gradually add water, processing for 2–3 minutes until smooth. Adjust consistency by adding water until mixture is slightly thicker than the consistency of heavy cream. Cover and set aside for 10 minutes.

2. In a deep-fat fryer or large pot over medium heat, heat oil to 350°F. Dip potato slices into batter one by one, and slip them into the fry oil in batches of six or seven. Fry for 4–5 minutes on each side, until golden brown and cooked through.

Per Serving

Calories: 86 | Fat: 4g | Sodium: 370mg
Carbohydrates: 9g | Fiber: 1g
Sugar: 1g | Protein: 2g

Spicy Rice Balls
YIELDS 30 RICE BALLS

Often called rice bombs at parties, these little bursts of flavor will make the guests come back for more.

Ingredients

4 cups hot cooked jasmine rice

2 tablespoons red curry paste

1 tablespoon soy sauce

1 tablespoon granulated sugar

2 kaffir lime leaves, cut into thin strips

3 cups vegetable oil

1. In a large bowl, combine rice, curry paste, soy sauce, sugar, and lime leaves. Taste and adjust seasoning. If the mixture is dry, add some water so it is easier to roll.

2. Wet your hands to prevent the mixture from sticking, then scoop 2 tablespoons mixture and roll into a round ball.

3. In a large pot or deep fryer over medium heat, heat oil to 350°F. Carefully drop rice balls into oil and fry until golden, about 2 minutes. Drain on paper towels.

Per Rice Ball

Calories: 51 | Fat: 2g | Sodium: 56mg
Carbohydrates: 7g | Fiber: 0g
Sugar: 0g | Protein: 1g

Tapioca Delight (Sabudana Vada)

SERVES 4

If you find the green chilies are too hot for your taste, remove the seeds before you cook with them. You'll get the flavor without the heat. One word of caution, though: Wear gloves when you seed the chilies.

Ingredients

1 cup uncooked tapioca

2 medium russet potatoes, peeled and diced into 1/2" cubes

2 medium green serrano chili peppers, minced with seeds

2 sprigs fresh cilantro, stemmed and minced

1/2 teaspoon salt

1/4 cup roughly ground unsalted dry-roasted peanuts

1 tablespoon freshly squeezed lemon juice

1 cup vegetable oil

1. In a large bowl, combine tapioca with enough water to cover, and soak for 3 hours. Drain off any remaining water and return tapioca to the bowl.

2. While tapioca is soaking, in a medium saucepan over medium-high heat, combine potatoes with enough water to cover. Bring to a boil and cook until just fork-tender, about 5–8 minutes. Drain potatoes and mash with a fork or potato masher. Add to drained tapioca.

3. Add serranos, cilantro, salt, peanuts, and lemon juice to potato mixture. Mix thoroughly with your hands.

4. Lightly oil your hands and form about 1/4 cup of the mixture into a ball, then flatten it into a small patty. Continue making patties until you have used up all the mixture.

5. In a large pot over medium heat, heat 1" oil to 350°F. Add one patty at a time and cook until golden brown, about 2 minutes per side. Remove patties from oil and drain on paper towels.

Per Serving

Calories: 362 | Fat: 17g | Sodium: 296mg
Carbohydrates: 46g | Fiber: 3g
Sugar: 3g | Protein: 4g

Chapter Five

SALADS

Spicy Southwestern Two-Bean Salad

SERVES 6

This cold bean salad with Tex-Mex flavors is even better the next day—if it lasts that long!

Ingredients

1 (15-ounce) can black beans, drained and rinsed

1 (15-ounce) can kidney beans, drained and rinsed

1 medium red bell pepper, stemmed, seeded, and chopped

1 large tomato, cored and diced

$\frac{2}{3}$ cup corn kernels

1 medium red onion, peeled and diced

$\frac{1}{3}$ cup olive oil

$\frac{1}{4}$ cup freshly squeezed lime juice

$\frac{1}{2}$ teaspoon chili powder

$\frac{1}{2}$ teaspoon garlic powder

$\frac{1}{4}$ teaspoon cayenne pepper

$\frac{1}{2}$ teaspoon salt

$\frac{1}{4}$ cup chopped fresh cilantro

1 medium avocado, peeled, pitted, and diced

1. In a large bowl, combine black beans, kidney beans, bell pepper, tomato, corn, and onion.

2. In a separate small bowl, whisk together olive oil, lime juice, chili powder, garlic powder, cayenne pepper, and salt until combined.

3. Pour dressing over bean mixture, tossing to coat. Stir in fresh cilantro.

4. Refrigerate for at least 1 hour before serving to allow flavors to blend.

5. Add avocado and gently toss again just before serving.

Per Serving

Calories: 303 | Fat: 16g | Sodium: 464mg
Carbohydrates: 32g | Fiber: 12g
Sugar: 4g | Protein: 10g

MAKE IT A PASTA SALAD
Omit the avocado and add some cooked whole-wheat pasta and extra dressing to turn this dish into a high-protein Tex-Mex pasta salad!

Sprouted Mung Bean Salad (Moong Dal Ka Salaad)

SERVES 4

If you don't like eating raw beans, you can either sauté them lightly or boil them in lightly salted water for about 2 minutes. Garnish with freshly chopped cilantro before serving.

Ingredients

1 medium clove garlic, peeled and crushed

½ medium English cucumber, peeled and finely diced

1 teaspoon grated fresh ginger

2 medium green serrano chili peppers, stemmed, seeded, and finely chopped

⅛ teaspoon salt

2 teaspoons freshly squeezed lemon juice

¼ teaspoon granulated sugar

1 cup sprouted mung beans (bean sprouts)

In a large salad bowl, combine all ingredients. Refrigerate for 20 minutes before serving to allow flavors to blend.

Per Serving

Calories: 12 | Fat: 0g | Sodium: 117mg
Carbohydrates: 3g | Fiber: 1g
Sugar: 2g | Protein: 1g

Cucumber-Cilantro Salad

SERVES 3

In this recipe, cooling cucumbers and cold, creamy yogurt are coupled with a dash of cayenne pepper for a salad that keeps you guessing.

Ingredients

4 medium cucumbers, peeled and diced

2 medium tomatoes, cored and chopped

$\frac{1}{2}$ medium red onion, peeled and diced small

1 cup plain soy yogurt

1 tablespoon freshly squeezed lemon juice

2 tablespoons chopped fresh cilantro

$\frac{1}{8}$ teaspoon salt

$\frac{1}{8}$ teaspoon black pepper

$\frac{1}{4}$ teaspoon cayenne pepper

1. In a large bowl, toss together all ingredients, stirring well to combine.

2. Refrigerate for at least 2 hours before serving to allow flavors to blend. Toss again just before serving.

Per Serving

Calories: 136 | Fat: 1g | Sodium: 121mg
Carbohydrates: 28g | Fiber: 4g
Sugar: 14g | Protein: 6g

Messy Taco Salad

SERVES 4

If you're bored by the usual salads but still want something light and green, try this taco salad. The taste and texture is best with iceberg lettuce, but if you want something more nutritious, use a blend of half iceberg and half romaine. Top with a handful of shredded vegan cheese if you'd like.

Ingredients

2 medium heads iceberg lettuce, cored and chopped

½ cup sliced black olives

½ cup corn kernels

1 medium jalapeño pepper, stemmed, seeded, and sliced

1 can vegetarian refried black beans

1 teaspoon hot sauce

¼ cup salsa

¼ cup vegan mayonnaise

12 corn tortilla chips, crumbled

1 medium avocado, peeled, pitted, and diced

1. In a large bowl, combine lettuce, olives, corn, and jalapeño.

2. In a small saucepan on medium heat, warm beans slightly, just until softened, about 3–4 minutes (or place beans in a medium microwave-safe bowl and microwave on high about 1 minute). Remove beans from heat and add hot sauce, salsa, and mayonnaise, breaking up the beans and mixing to form a thick sauce.

3. Add bean mixture to lettuce mixture, stirring to combine as much as possible. Fold in tortilla chips and avocado, and stir gently to combine.

Per Serving

Calories: 361 | Fat: 19g | Sodium: 899mg
Carbohydrates: 36g | Fiber: 12g
Sugar: 8g | Protein: 10g

BAKED TORTILLA CHIPS

Why not make your own tortilla chips? Slice whole-wheat tortillas into strips or triangles, and arrange in a single layer on a baking sheet. Drizzle with olive oil for a crispier chip, and season with a bit of salt and garlic powder if you want, or just bake them plain. It'll take about 5–6 minutes on each side in a 300°F oven.

Spicy Sweet Cucumber Salad

SERVES 2

This Japanese cucumber salad is cool and refreshing, but with a bit of spice. Enjoy it as a healthy afternoon snack, or as a fresh accompaniment to takeout.

Ingredients

2 medium cucumbers, peeled, trimmed, and thinly sliced

$3/4$ teaspoon salt

$1/4$ cup rice vinegar

1 tablespoon agave nectar

1 teaspoon sesame oil

$1/4$ teaspoon red pepper flakes

$1/2$ medium yellow onion, peeled and thinly sliced

1. In a large, shallow container or on a baking sheet, spread cucumbers in a single layer and sprinkle with salt. Allow to sit for at least 10 minutes.

2. Drain any excess water from cucumbers and add them to a large bowl.

3. In a separate small bowl, whisk together vinegar, agave, oil, and red pepper flakes until combined.

4. Pour dressing over cucumbers, add onion, and toss gently.

5. Allow to sit at least 10 minutes at room temperature before serving to allow flavors to blend.

Per Serving

Calories: 102 | Fat: 2g | Sodium: 880mg
Carbohydrates: 19g | Fiber: 2g
Sugar: 11g | Protein: 2g

Lemon-Cumin Potato Salad
SERVES 4

A mayonnaise-free potato salad with exotic flavors, this spicy dish is delicious either hot or cold.

Ingredients

2 tablespoons olive oil

1 small yellow onion, peeled and diced

1½ teaspoons ground cumin

4 large cooked russet potatoes, peeled and chopped

3 tablespoons freshly squeezed lemon juice

2 teaspoons Dijon mustard

1 medium scallion, trimmed and chopped

¼ teaspoon cayenne pepper

2 tablespoons chopped fresh cilantro

1. In a large skillet over medium-high heat, add oil and sauté onion until soft, about 5 minutes. Add cumin and potatoes, and cook for just 1 minute, stirring well to combine. Remove from heat.

2. In a small bowl, whisk together lemon juice and mustard, and pour over potatoes, tossing gently to coat. Add scallion, cayenne pepper, and cilantro, and combine well.

3. Serve hot or refrigerate before serving.

Per Serving

Calories: 226 | Fat: 7g | Sodium: 74mg
Carbohydrates: 37g | Fiber: 3g
Sugar: 4g | Protein: 4g

THE FAMILY RECIPE

Traditional American potato salads are easy to veganize, so if you have a family favorite, take a look at the ingredients. Substitute vegan mayonnaise or sour cream for regular, omit the eggs, and use mock meats in place of the bacon bits or other meats.

Asian Cucumber Salad

SERVES 4

This refreshing, crisp dish is the perfect counterbalance with grilled tempeh, spicy corn fritters, and other hearty fare. Garnish with chopped red onion if you like.

Ingredients

1/4 cup rice vinegar

1 teaspoon sugar

1 small jalapeño pepper, stemmed, seeded, and finely chopped

1 large cucumber, peeled and thinly sliced lengthwise

1/8 teaspoon sesame oil

1. Whisk together rice vinegar, sugar, and chopped jalapeño. Combine cucumber with dressing, drizzle in sesame oil, and toss to coat.

2. Marinate for at least 10 minutes before serving.

Per Serving

Calories: 19 | Fat: 0g | Sodium: 1mg
Carbohydrates: 4g | Fiber: 0g
Sugar: 2g | Protein: 1g

Red Onion Salad (Rani Pyaz)
SERVES 4

These Indian pickles have a short shelf life of about a week, so use them up quickly. Use a few drops of red food coloring to give this dish an authentic look.

Ingredients

1 cup frozen pearl onions, thawed

2½ cups water, divided

½ cup distilled white vinegar

½ teaspoon ground black mustard seeds

1 medium green serrano chili pepper, stemmed, seeded, and chopped

½ teaspoon salt

1. In a small saucepan over medium-high heat, combine onions and 2 cups water. Bring to a boil and cook until tender, about 5–7 minutes. Drain and set aside.

2. In a large, deep pot over medium-high heat, bring vinegar and remaining water to a boil. Remove from heat and set aside.

3. In a medium bowl, combine onions, mustard seeds, serrano, and salt; mix well. Pour vinegar mixture over onion mixture.

4. Cool and transfer to an airtight container. Refrigerate for 48 hours before eating to allow flavors to blend.

Per Serving

Calories: 11 | Fat: 0g | Sodium: 32mg
Carbohydrates: 2g | Fiber: 0g
Sugar: 1g | Protein: 0g

Black Bean and Barley Taco Salad

SERVES 2

Adding barley to a taco salad gives a bit of a whole-grain fiber boost to this low-fat, spicy recipe.

Ingredients

1 (15-ounce) can black beans, drained and rinsed

1/2 teaspoon ground cumin

1/2 teaspoon dried oregano

2 tablespoons freshly squeezed lime juice

1 teaspoon hot sauce

1 cup cooked barley

1 medium head iceberg lettuce, cored and shredded

3/4 cup salsa

1/2 cup corn tortilla chips, crumbled

2 tablespoons vegan Italian dressing

1. In a medium bowl, mash together beans, cumin, oregano, lime juice, and hot sauce until beans are mostly mashed, then combine with barley.

2. In a large salad bowl, layer lettuce with beans and barley. Top with salsa and tortilla chips. Drizzle with Italian dressing.

Per Serving

Calories: 425 | Fat: 5g | Sodium: 1,438mg
Carbohydrates: 79g | Fiber: 24g
Sugar: 14g | Protein: 18g

Curried "Chicken" Salad

SERVES 3

Turn this spicy "chicken" salad into a sandwich, or slice up some tomatoes and serve on a bed of lettuce.

Ingredients

1 (8-ounce) package tempeh, diced small

3 tablespoons vegan mayonnaise

2 teaspoons freshly squeezed lemon juice

½ teaspoon garlic powder

1 teaspoon Dijon mustard

2 tablespoons sweet pickle relish

½ cup green peas

2 medium stalks celery, trimmed and finely diced

½ teaspoon curry powder

⅛ teaspoon cayenne pepper

⅛ teaspoon black pepper

1. In a medium saucepan over medium heat, combine tempeh with enough water to cover. Simmer until tempeh is soft, about 10 minutes. Drain and allow to cool completely. Transfer to a large bowl.

2. In a small bowl, whisk together mayonnaise, lemon juice, garlic powder, mustard, and relish until combined.

3. Combine mayonnaise mixture with tempeh, peas, celery, curry powder, cayenne pepper, and black pepper. Gently toss to combine.

4. Refrigerate for at least 1 hour before serving to allow flavors to blend.

Per Serving

Calories: 274 | Fat: 16g | Sodium: 264mg
Carbohydrates: 15g | Fiber: 2g
Sugar: 2g | Protein: 16g

Spiced Couscous Salad

SERVES 4

This salad can act as a full meal for lunch or dinner, or a side salad, depending on how hungry you are!

Ingredients

2 cups Vegetable Broth
(see recipe in Chapter 6)

2 cups uncooked couscous

1 teaspoon ground cumin

$\frac{1}{2}$ teaspoon turmeric

$\frac{1}{2}$ teaspoon paprika

$\frac{1}{4}$ teaspoon cayenne pepper

1 tablespoon freshly squeezed
lemon juice

2 tablespoons olive oil

2 medium zucchini, trimmed
and sliced

1 medium red bell pepper, stemmed,
seeded, and chopped

1 medium yellow bell pepper,
stemmed, seeded, and chopped

3 medium cloves garlic, peeled
and minced

2 tablespoons chopped fresh parsley

$\frac{1}{8}$ teaspoon salt

$\frac{1}{8}$ teaspoon black pepper

1. In a medium saucepan over medium-high heat, combine Vegetable Broth and couscous. Bring to a boil and add cumin, turmeric, paprika, and cayenne pepper, and stir to combine.

2. Turn off heat, cover, and allow to sit until couscous is soft and liquid is absorbed, at least 15 minutes. Fluff couscous with a fork and add lemon juice.

3. In a large skillet over medium-high heat, add oil and sauté zucchini, bell peppers, and garlic just until soft, about 5 minutes. Add couscous, parsley, salt, and black pepper; taste and adjust seasonings.

Per Serving

Calories: 434 | Fat: 7g | Sodium: 95mg
Carbohydrates: 77g | Fiber: 7g
Sugar: 4g | Protein: 13g

Southeast Asian Slaw

SERVES 4

This crisp, lightly spiced salad is fine enough to roll in Asian-inspired wraps, and it combines beautifully with jasmine rice cooked in coconut milk for a unique flavor. To shred the cabbage as fine as possible, use a mandoline or slicing machine.

Ingredients

¼ head (about ½ pound) Napa cabbage, cored and shredded very fine

½ medium carrot, peeled and grated

1 small red onion, peeled and julienne sliced

1 small jalapeño pepper, stemmed, seeded, and finely chopped

¼ cup chopped fresh cilantro

2 tablespoons freshly squeezed lime juice

1 tablespoon rice vinegar

1 teaspoon granulated sugar

1 teaspoon vegetable oil

⅛ teaspoon sesame oil

½ teaspoon salt

1. In a large bowl, combine shredded cabbage with carrot, onion, jalapeño, and cilantro.

2. In a small bowl, whisk together lime juice, vinegar, sugar, vegetable oil, sesame oil, and salt until combined. Add to cabbage mixture and toss thoroughly.

3. Refrigerate for at least 30 minutes before serving to allow flavors to blend.

Per Serving

Calories: 47 | Fat: 1g | Sodium: 310mg
Carbohydrates: 9g | Fiber: 2g
Sugar: 4g | Protein: 1g

Lentil Salad
SERVES 8

One of the oldest foods known to man, lentils have been found among the remains of prehistoric communities and are mentioned in the earliest books of the Bible. They cook more quickly than other beans, never require soaking, and taste great with the spicy flavors found in this Lentil Salad. Serve with a bed of dressed baby greens.

Ingredients

1 pound dried lentils

2 quarts water

2 medium yellow onions, finely chopped

3 medium scallions, trimmed and chopped

1 medium green bell pepper, stemmed, seeded, and finely chopped

1 tablespoon roasted ground cumin

$\frac{1}{8}$ teaspoon cayenne pepper

$\frac{1}{4}$ cup freshly squeezed lemon juice

2 tablespoons olive oil

$\frac{1}{8}$ teaspoon salt

$\frac{1}{8}$ teaspoon black pepper

1. In a large saucepan over medium-high heat, add lentils and water. Cover and bring to a boil. Reduce heat to low and simmer until tender but not broken up, about 15–20 minutes. Drain and spread on a pan to cool completely.

2. In a large bowl, combine cooled lentils with onions, scallions, and bell pepper.

3. In a separate small bowl, whisk together cumin, cayenne pepper, lemon juice, oil, salt, and black pepper to combine. Pour over lentil mixture and toss thoroughly.

Per Serving

Calories: 251 | Fat: 4g | Sodium: 43mg
Carbohydrates: 39g | Fiber: 15g
Sugar: 5g | Protein: 16g

Shiitake Mushroom Salad with Chilies
SERVES 4

This is a simple, spicy, plant-based dish with plenty of heat and earthy mushroom flavor. Garnish with extra chilies and scallions if you like.

Ingredients

12 medium dried chilies de árbol, stemmed and seeded

2 tablespoons thinly sliced scallions (including both green and white parts)

2 tablespoons sesame oil

2 tablespoons rice vinegar

2 tablespoons soy sauce

1 teaspoon salt

12 large shiitake mushrooms, stemmed and thinly sliced

1. In a spice grinder or food processor, grind chilies until they make a fine powder. Transfer to a small bowl and add scallions, oil, vinegar, and soy sauce. Set dressing aside.

2. Fill a medium saucepan with water and salt, and set over high heat. Bring to a boil. Add mushrooms and cook until lightly chewy, about 4–5 minutes.

3. Drain mushrooms well. Transfer them to a kitchen towel or paper towels and squeeze out as much liquid as possible.

4. Put mushrooms in a medium bowl and pour dressing over top. Toss and let stand for 10 minutes before serving to allow flavors to blend.

Per Serving

Calories: 102 | Fat: 7g | Sodium: 569mg
Carbohydrates: 8g | Fiber: 1g
Sugar: 2g | Protein: 2g

SHIITAKE MUSHROOMS

Of the many varieties of mushrooms around the world, shiitakes are most strongly associated with Asian cuisine. They're used throughout Japanese, Chinese, and Korean cooking. Pronounced "she-TAH-kay," the name is derived from the Japanese word for *tree*. They have a very strong, earthy flavor. You can find them fresh at most grocery stores, and also dried at many Asian markets.

Punjabi Onion Salad (Punjabi Laccha)

SERVES 4

Add chaat masala, an Indian spice blend, to this plant-based dish instead of salt for a unique tangy flavor.

Ingredients

1 medium red onion, peeled and sliced into rings

2 medium green serrano chili peppers, stemmed, seeded, and sliced

1 tablespoon freshly squeezed lemon juice

1/8 teaspoon salt

1/2 teaspoon minced fresh cilantro

Arrange onion rings on a platter. Top with serranos, then sprinkle with lemon juice and salt. Garnish with cilantro and serve.

Per Serving

Calories: 12 | Fat: 0g | Sodium: 73mg
Carbohydrates: 3g | Fiber: 1g
Sugar: 1g | Protein: 0g

Chipotle–Black Bean Salad

SERVES 8

There are actually five different varieties of black beans, but when you purchase them, they are often just labeled as "black beans." No matter what type of black beans you buy, they'll cook up great in the slow cooker for this spicy, fresh salad!

Ingredients

1 (16-ounce) bag dried black beans, rinsed and soaked overnight

2 teaspoons salt

1 tablespoon chipotle chili powder

2 teaspoons dried thyme

2 medium tomatoes, cored and diced

1 medium red onion, peeled and diced

$\frac{1}{4}$ cup chopped fresh cilantro

1. In a large saucepan over medium-high heat, combine beans with enough water to cover and bring to a boil. Boil for 10 minutes.

2. Drain beans and transfer to a 4-quart slow cooker. Add salt and enough water to cover beans by 1". Cover and cook on high until beans are tender, about 5–6 hours.

3. Once beans are done, drain in a colander and allow to cool to room temperature. Transfer to a large bowl.

4. Mix in remaining ingredients and serve.

Per Serving

Calories: 212 | Fat: 1g | Sodium: 420mg
Carbohydrates: 39g | Fiber: 14g
Sugar: 1g | Protein: 14g

PREPPING DRIED BEANS

Before cooking with dried beans, you must first rinse them, soak them overnight in a pot full of water, and then boil them for 10 minutes. They are then ready for step 2 of the recipe.

Tunisian Fried Pepper Salad

SERVES 6

This salad, which is also known as marmouma or chakchouka, makes an unexpected but delightful side dish or appetizer. Feel free to turn up the heat with more hot paprika. Serve it with crusty bread and, if you like, vegan goat cheese.

Ingredients

4 tablespoons olive oil

4 medium red bell peppers, stemmed, seeded, and cut into ½" pieces

5 medium cloves garlic, peeled and finely chopped

1½ pounds tomatoes, cored and roughly chopped

1 teaspoon hot paprika

⅛ teaspoon salt

⅛ teaspoon black pepper

1. In a large skillet over medium heat, add oil and sauté bell peppers until soft, about 5 minutes.

2. Add garlic and cook until garlic is softened and the peppers are lightly browned, about 5 minutes.

3. Add tomatoes, paprika, salt, and black pepper. Give the whole mixture a gentle stir and then simmer, uncovered, until tomatoes are reduced to a very thick consistency, about 20–25 minutes.

Per Serving

Calories: 127 | Fat: 9g | Sodium: 57mg
Carbohydrates: 10g | Fiber: 3g
Sugar: 6g | Protein: 2g

Shredded Carrot Salad (Gajar Ka Salaad)

SERVES 4

This brightly colored Indian salad is a perfect side dish or main course!

Ingredients

2 cups shredded carrots

2 tablespoons unsalted dry-roasted peanuts, roughly chopped

1 medium green serrano chili pepper, stemmed, seeded, and minced

2 tablespoons freshly squeezed lemon juice

1 tablespoon vegetable oil

$\frac{1}{2}$ teaspoon black mustard seeds

$\frac{1}{8}$ teaspoon salt

1. In a large bowl, combine carrots, peanuts, serrano, and lemon juice; mix well. Set aside.

2. In a small skillet over medium-high heat, add oil and mustard seeds. When the seeds begin to crackle, remove from heat and pour over the carrots.

3. Add salt and mix well. Serve immediately.

Per Serving

Calories: 83 | Fat: 6g | Sodium: 110mg
Carbohydrates: 7g | Fiber: 2g
Sugar: 3g | Protein: 2g

Black Bean Salad with Tapatío Vinaigrette

SERVES 6

Tapatío, cilantro, black beans, and cumin give this salad a fresh but decidedly south-of-the-border flavor. Adjust the amount of hot sauce to your liking for more or less heat.

Ingredients

¼ cup freshly squeezed lime juice

¼ teaspoon salt

1 teaspoon Tapatío hot sauce

1 medium clove garlic, peeled and finely minced

¼ teaspoon ground cumin

¾ cup olive oil

1 cup quinoa, cooked according to package directions

1 (15-ounce) can black beans, drained and rinsed

½ medium red onion, peeled and finely chopped

2 cups quartered cherry tomatoes

1 large carrot, peeled and finely chopped

⅓ cup chopped fresh cilantro

1. In a small bowl or jar, combine lime juice, salt, Tapatío, garlic, cumin, and oil. Stir or shake to combine. Taste and adjust seasonings to your liking.

2. In a large bowl, combine cooked quinoa, black beans, onion, tomatoes, carrot, and cilantro. Stir to mix well.

3. Toss salad with ¼ cup of the Tapatío vinaigrette. Taste and adjust seasonings to your liking, adding more dressing, cumin, salt, or black pepper as needed.

Per Serving

Calories: 364 | Fat: 27g | Sodium: 298mg
Carbohydrates: 24g | Fiber: 7g
Sugar: 3g | Protein: 7g

QUINOA

Quinoa (pronounced "KEEN-wah") is a plant that has been cultivated in the Andes mountains of South America since 3000 B.C. Ancient Incas called quinoa "the mother grain." It has a nutty flavor, and varieties come in colors ranging from tan to red to black. Quinoa is growing in popularity, likely because it is highly nutritious. It can be used as a substitute for grains like rice, but it contains high amounts of fiber.

Cactus Salad

SERVES 2

Cactus leaves, called *nopales*, are a common salad ingredient in Mexico. They have a distinct crunch and texture similar to okra. If you're not sure about handling fresh nopales, you can also buy them jarred at most Mexican or specialty groceries.

Ingredients

2 large nopal (cactus) pads, thorns and bumps removed, cut into bite-sized pieces

$1/4$ teaspoon salt, divided

$1/2$ large white onion, peeled and diced

2 medium tomatoes, cored and cubed

4 medium sprigs fresh cilantro, finely chopped

2 medium jalapeño peppers, seeded and finely chopped

1 medium avocado, peeled, pitted, and cubed

2 tablespoons freshly squeezed lime juice

$1/8$ teaspoon black pepper

1. Fill a medium saucepan with water and set over medium-high heat. Bring to a boil and add nopales and $1/8$ teaspoon salt. Boil until tender, about 25 minutes. Drain well.

2. Transfer nopales to a large bowl. Add all remaining ingredients, then stir gently until thoroughly mixed.

3. Refrigerate until salad is cooled.

Per Serving

Calories: 176 | Fat: 10g | Sodium: 193mg
Carbohydrates: 20g | Fiber: 9g
Sugar: 7g | Protein: 5g

Mango Salad
SERVES 3

Green mangoes are the best for this Thai salad. They can be purchased at Asian grocery stores from April to September. Carrots or cucumbers can be used for this recipe, and green apples make an excellent substitution for mangoes if necessary. Garnish with extra chopped cilantro if you like.

Ingredients

2 cups julienned green mangoes

¼ cup thinly sliced shallot

¼ cup chopped unsalted dry-roasted almonds

2 tablespoons chopped fresh cilantro

3 tablespoons freshly squeezed lime juice

3 tablespoons vegan fish sauce

2 medium Thai (bird's eye) chili peppers, stemmed, seeded, and minced

1 teaspoon granulated sugar

In a large bowl, toss all ingredients together to combine. Refrigerate for at least 30 minutes before serving to allow flavors to blend.

Per Serving

Calories: 176 | Fat: 5g | Sodium: 1,049mg
Carbohydrates: 30g | Fiber: 4g
Sugar: 7g | Protein: 5g

Tempeh Salad
SERVES 4

Tempeh is a traditional soy product originally from Indonesia. It is made using a natural culturing and controlled fermentation process that binds soybeans into cake form.

Dressing Ingredients

3 medium Thai (bird's eye) chili peppers, stemmed, seeded, and chopped

3 tablespoons soy sauce

1/4 cup freshly squeezed lime juice

1 tablespoon granulated sugar

Salad Ingredients

8 ounces fresh tempeh, cubed and deep-fried

1 medium pickling cucumber, quartered lengthwise and sliced

1 medium tomato, cored and chopped

1/4 cup chopped fresh cilantro

1/4 cup chopped scallions

1. In a small bowl, combine all dressing ingredients. Whisk until sugar is dissolved.

2. In a large bowl, combine all salad ingredients with the dressing and toss to combine.

Per Serving

Calories: 217 | Fat: 11g | Sodium: 675mg
Carbohydrates: 19g | Fiber: 2g
Sugar: 8g | Protein: 13g

Mixed Vegetables with Hot Pepper Dressing

SERVES 6

Experiment by adding smoked or pickled peppers to the dressing instead of fresh peppers.

Ingredients

1 cup chopped broccoli florets

1 cup chopped cauliflower florets

1 cup halved fresh green beans

1 large carrot, peeled and cut into ¼" rounds

4 medium radishes, trimmed and cut into ¼" rounds

½ cup quartered pimiento-stuffed green olives

1 cup canned corn kernels, drained

2 large tomatoes, cored and cut into thin wedges

2 medium serrano chili peppers, stemmed (not seeded) and minced

2 medium cloves garlic, peeled and minced

1 cup dry red wine

1 cup olive oil

½ teaspoon dried oregano

½ teaspoon salt

½ teaspoon cayenne pepper

1. In a large bowl, combine broccoli, cauliflower, beans, carrot, radishes, olives, corn, and tomatoes.

2. In a small container or jar with a cover, combine serranos, garlic, red wine, and oil. Add the oregano, salt, and cayenne pepper. Cover and shake until well mixed.

3. Pour dressing over vegetables; toss gently until well mixed.

4. Refrigerate to allow flavors to blend for the best flavor.

Per Serving

Calories: 435 | Fat: 38g | Sodium: 571mg
Carbohydrates: 14g | Fiber: 4g
Sugar: 5g | Protein: 3g

WHAT HAPPENED TO THE SALAD?

Mexicans typically don't serve a salad course with their meals. If a green salad is served, it typically takes the place of the vegetable. As a result, many of their salads feature a wide variety of vegetables.

Sesame-Potato Salad (Til Aur Aloo Ka Salaad)

SERVES 4

Serve with Indian flatbread such as naan or rotis, or enjoy by itself! Add a few drops of red food coloring before serving to make this plant-based dish really stand out.

Ingredients

4 medium russet potatoes, peeled and chopped into ½" dice

½ teaspoon plus ⅛ teaspoon salt, divided

1 medium green serrano chili pepper, stemmed, seeded, and minced

1 tablespoon sesame seeds, roasted

2 tablespoons freshly squeezed lemon juice

2 tablespoons warm water

1 medium dried red chili, roughly pounded

½ teaspoon black pepper

1 teaspoon finely chopped fresh cilantro

1. Fill a medium saucepan with water and set over medium-high heat. Add ½ teaspoon salt and potatoes and boil, covered, until just fork-tender, 5–8 minutes. Drain.

2. In a large bowl, combine potatoes, serrano, sesame seeds, lemon juice, and ⅛ teaspoon salt; mix well. Add warm water and toss well.

3. When you are ready to serve, sprinkle with dried red chili, black pepper, and cilantro. Serve immediately.

Per Serving

Calories: 170 | Fat: 1g | Sodium: 476mg
Carbohydrates: 37g | Fiber: 5g
Sugar: 2g | Protein: 4g

Chapter Six

SOUPS, STEWS, AND CHILIS

Vegetable Broth

YIELDS 4 CUPS

This versatile Vegetable Broth is not really spicy, but it can be used as the base for almost any soup or stew.

Ingredients

2 large yellow onions, peeled and halved

2 medium carrots, peeled and cut into large pieces

3 medium stalks celery, trimmed and cut in half

1 medium head garlic, cloves separated, peeled, and crushed

10 peppercorns

1 bay leaf

6 cups water

1. In a 4-quart slow cooker, combine all ingredients. Cover and cook on low for 8–10 hours.

2. Strain Vegetable Broth; discard vegetables. Store in the refrigerator.

Per 1 Cup

Calories: 5 | Fat: 0g | Sodium: 4mg
Carbohydrates: 1g | Fiber: 0g
Sugar: 1g | Protein: 0g

STORING BROTH
Homemade Vegetable Broth can be refrigerated in a covered container for 2–3 days, or frozen for up to 3 months.

Red Lentil Soup

SERVES 6

This spicy soup is perfect for lunch or as a dinner starter. If you want to spice it up even more, just add more cayenne pepper.

Ingredients

3 tablespoons olive oil

1 small yellow onion, peeled and sliced

1½ teaspoons minced fresh ginger

2 medium cloves garlic, peeled and minced

2 cups dried red lentils

6 cups Vegetable Broth (see recipe in this chapter)

¼ cup freshly squeezed lemon juice

½ teaspoon paprika

1 teaspoon cayenne pepper

1½ teaspoons salt

1. In a medium skillet over medium heat, add oil and sauté onion, ginger, and garlic until soft, about 5 minutes. Transfer to a 4-quart slow cooker.

2. Add all remaining ingredients. Cover and cook on low for 6–8 hours, until the lentils are tender.

Per Serving

Calories: 265 | Fat: 7g | Sodium: 589mg
Carbohydrates: 37g | Fiber: 13g
Sugar: 5g | Protein: 15g

CLEANING LENTILS

Before cooking lentils, place them in a colander and run ample cold water over them to rinse thoroughly. Sort through the bunch to remove and discard any debris or small stones that may be lingering behind.

Black Bean Soup

SERVES 6

You can use the leftover red onion from this spicy recipe to make Fajita Chili (see recipe in this chapter).

Ingredients

2 tablespoons olive oil

½ medium green bell pepper, stemmed, seeded, and diced

½ medium red bell pepper, stemmed, seeded, and diced

½ medium red onion, peeled and sliced

2 medium cloves garlic, peeled and minced

2 (15-ounce) cans black beans, drained and rinsed

2 teaspoons cumin seeds, minced

1 teaspoon chipotle chili powder

1 teaspoon salt

4 cups Vegetable Broth (see recipe in this chapter)

¼ cup chopped fresh cilantro

1. In a large skillet over medium heat, add oil and sauté bell peppers, onion, and garlic until slightly softened, 2–3 minutes. Transfer to a 4-quart slow cooker.

2. Add beans, cumin, chipotle powder, salt, and Vegetable Broth. Cover and cook on low for 6 hours.

3. Let the soup cool slightly, then pour half into a blender. Process until smooth, then pour back into the pot. Stir in cilantro.

Per Serving

Calories: 182 | Fat: 5g | Sodium: 709mg
Carbohydrates: 26g | Fiber: 10g
Sugar: 1g | Protein: 9g

Chinese Hot and Sour Soup

SERVES 6

If this Americanized version of hot and sour soup just doesn't satisfy your Szechuan cravings, hit up a specialty Asian grocery store and replace the cabbage with ½ cup dried lily buds and substitute half of the shiitake with wood ear fungus.

Ingredients

2 tablespoons vegetable oil

2 cups finely diced traditional seitan

1½ teaspoons hot sauce

6 cups Vegetable Broth (see recipe in this chapter)

½ medium head Napa cabbage, cored and shredded

¾ cup sliced shiitake mushrooms

1 (8-ounce) can bamboo shoots, drained

2 tablespoons soy sauce

2 tablespoons distilled white vinegar

¾ teaspoon red pepper flakes

¾ teaspoon salt

2 tablespoons cornstarch

¼ cup water

3 medium scallions, trimmed and sliced

2 teaspoons chili oil

1. In a large skillet over medium-high heat, add oil and sauté seitan until cooked, about 2–3 minutes. Reduce heat to low and add hot sauce, stirring well to coat. Cook for 1 more minute, then remove from heat and set aside.

2. In a large soup pot or stockpot over medium heat, combine Vegetable Broth, cabbage, mushrooms, bamboo shoots, soy sauce, vinegar, red pepper flakes, and salt. Bring to a slow simmer and cover. Simmer for at least 15 minutes.

3. In a separate small bowl, whisk together the cornstarch and water, then slowly stir into soup. Heat just until soup thickens.

4. Top each serving with scallions and drizzle with chili oil.

Per Serving

Calories: 196 | Fat: 6g | Sodium: 897mg
Carbohydrates: 18g | Fiber: 4g
Sugar: 6g | Protein: 18g

Tortilla Soup
SERVES 8

Turn this spicy soup into a complete meal by adding pieces of cooked vegan chicken, such as Morningstar Farms Veggie Chik'n Strips or Gardein Meatless Chick'n Strips.

Ingredients

2 tablespoons olive oil

1 large yellow onion, peeled and chopped

2 medium cloves garlic, peeled and minced

2 tablespoons soy sauce

7 cups Vegetable Broth (see recipe in this chapter)

1 (16-ounce) package firm silken tofu, crumbled

2 cups diced tomatoes

1 cup corn kernels

1 teaspoon chipotle chili powder

1 teaspoon cayenne pepper

2 teaspoons ground cumin

2 teaspoons salt

1 teaspoon dried oregano

10 (6") corn tortillas, sliced into strips

2 cups (8 ounces) shredded vegan Cheddar cheese

1. In a medium skillet over medium heat, add oil and sauté onion until soft, about 5 minutes. Add garlic and sauté for an additional 30 seconds. Transfer to a 4-quart slow cooker.

2. Add all remaining ingredients except tortillas and cheese, and stir to combine. Cover and cook on low for 4 hours.

3. While soup is cooking, preheat oven to 450°F. Place tortilla strips on an ungreased baking sheet. Bake for about 10 minutes, or until they turn golden brown. Remove from oven and set aside.

4. After soup has cooled slightly, use an immersion blender or regular blender to purée the soup.

5. Serve each bowl of soup topped with cooked tortilla strips and ¼ cup shredded cheese.

Per Serving

Calories: 259 | Fat: 14g | Sodium: 1,122mg
Carbohydrates: 30g | Fiber: 5g
Sugar: 5g | Protein: 8g

CHIPOTLE CHILI POWDER
Chipotle chili powder is made from ground chipotle peppers, a type of dried jalapeño. It brings a smoky spiciness to dishes but can be replaced with cayenne pepper or regular chili powder.

Cold Spanish Gazpacho with Avocado

SERVES 6

This gazpacho is best enjoyed on an outdoor patio just after sunset on a warm summer evening. But really, anytime you want a simple, spicy starter soup, this will do, no matter the weather. Add some crunch by topping with homemade croutons.

Ingredients

2 medium cucumbers, peeled and diced

1/2 medium red onion, peeled and diced

2 large tomatoes, cored and diced

1/4 cup chopped fresh cilantro

2 medium avocados, peeled, pitted, and diced

4 medium cloves garlic, peeled

2 tablespoons freshly squeezed lime juice

1 tablespoon red wine vinegar

3/4 cup Vegetable Broth (see recipe in this chapter)

1 medium serrano chili pepper

1/8 teaspoon salt

1/8 teaspoon black pepper

1. In a large bowl, combine cucumbers, onion, tomatoes, cilantro, and avocados. Pour half the mixture into a blender. Add garlic, lime juice, vinegar, Vegetable Broth, and serrano. Blend until smooth.

2. Pour blended vegetables back into bowl with chopped vegetables. Stir to combine.

3. Season with salt and black pepper.

Per Serving

Calories: 113 | Fat: 6g | Sodium: 60mg
Carbohydrates: 13g | Fiber: 5g
Sugar: 4g | Protein: 3g

CRUNCHY CROUTONS

Slice your favorite vegan artisan bread, focaccia, or whatever you've got into 1" cubes. Toss them in a large bowl with a generous coating of olive oil or a flavored oil, a bit of salt, and some Italian seasoning, garlic powder, a dash of cayenne pepper, or whatever you prefer. Transfer to a baking sheet and bake 15–20 minutes at 275°F, tossing once or twice.

Kidney Bean and Zucchini Gumbo

SERVES 5

Traditional gumbo always calls for filé powder, but if you can't find this anywhere, increase the amounts of the other spices—especially the Cajun seasoning—to give this plant-based dish even more of a kick. This vegetable gumbo uses zucchini instead of okra.

Ingredients

2 tablespoons olive oil

1 medium yellow onion, peeled and diced

1 medium red bell pepper, stemmed, seeded, and chopped

3 medium stalks celery, trimmed and chopped

1 medium zucchini, trimmed and sliced

1 (14-ounce) can diced tomatoes, undrained

3 cups Vegetable Broth (see recipe in this chapter)

1 teaspoon hot sauce

1 teaspoon filé powder

$3/4$ teaspoon dried thyme

1 teaspoon Cajun seasoning

2 bay leaves

1 (15-ounce) can kidney beans, drained and rinsed

$1^1/_2$ cups cooked brown rice

1. In a large soup pot or stockpot over medium-high heat, add oil and sauté onion, bell pepper, and celery until slightly softened, about 1–2 minutes. Reduce heat to low and add remaining ingredients except beans and rice.

2. Bring to a simmer, cover, and allow to cook for 30 minutes.

3. Uncover, add beans, and stir to combine. Heat for 5 more minutes. Remove bay leaves before serving. Serve over cooked rice.

Per Serving

Calories: 229 | Fat: 6g | Sodium: 364mg
Carbohydrates: 35g | Fiber: 8g
Sugar: 6g | Protein: 8g

GUMBO ON THE GO

If you don't have precooked rice on hand, add $2/3$ cup instant brown rice and an extra cup of Vegetable Broth during the last 10 minutes of cooking. For a "meatier texture," quickly brown some vegan sausage or ground beef substitute and toss it in the mix.

African Peanut and Greens Soup
SERVES 4

Reduce the liquids in this soup to turn it into a thick and chunky curry to pour over rice. Although the ingredients are all familiar, this is definitely not a boring meal!

Ingredients

2 tablespoons olive oil

1 medium yellow onion, peeled and diced

3 medium tomatoes, cored and chopped

2 cups Vegetable Broth (see recipe in this chapter)

1 cup canned coconut milk

$1/3$ cup peanut butter

1 (15-ounce) can chickpeas, drained and rinsed

$1/2$ teaspoon salt

1 teaspoon curry powder

1 teaspoon granulated sugar

$1/3$ teaspoon red pepper flakes

2 cups spinach, stems trimmed

1. In a large pot over medium-high heat, add oil and sauté onion and tomatoes until onion is soft, about 5 minutes.

2. Reduce heat to medium-low and add remaining ingredients except spinach, stirring well to combine.

3. Allow to simmer uncovered on low heat, stirring occasionally until mixture has thickened, about 8–10 minutes.

4. Add spinach and allow to cook just until spinach is wilted, another 1–2 minutes.

5. Remove from heat. Soup will thicken as it cools.

Per Serving

Calories: 423 | Fat: 30g | Sodium: 451mg
Carbohydrates: 29g | Fiber: 8g
Sugar: 9g | Protein: 13g

Jamaican Red Bean Stew
SERVES 4

Make your own hot and spicy jerk seasoning by combining thyme, allspice, black pepper, cinnamon, cayenne pepper, onion powder, and nutmeg.

Ingredients

2 tablespoons olive oil

1/2 medium yellow onion, peeled and diced

2 medium cloves garlic, peeled and minced

1 (15-ounce) can diced tomatoes, undrained

3 cups peeled and diced sweet potatoes

2 (15-ounce) cans red kidney beans, drained and rinsed

1 cup canned coconut milk

3 cups Vegetable Broth (see recipe in this chapter)

2 teaspoons jerk seasoning

2 teaspoons curry powder

1/8 teaspoon salt

1/8 teaspoon black pepper

1. In a skillet over medium heat, add oil and sauté onion and garlic until slightly softened, about 3 minutes. Transfer to a 4-quart slow cooker.

2. Add all remaining ingredients. Cover and cook on low for 6 hours.

Per Serving

Calories: 514 | Fat: 19g | Sodium: 691mg
Carbohydrates: 70g | Fiber: 18g
Sugar: 14g | Protein: 17g

Étouffée

SERVES 6

You can purchase the vegan shrimp used in this spicy dish online at https://veganessentials.com.

Ingredients

8 tablespoons vegan margarine

1 medium yellow onion, peeled and diced

3 medium stalks celery, trimmed and chopped

1 medium carrot, peeled and diced

3 medium cloves garlic, peeled and minced

1 medium green bell pepper, stemmed, seeded, and chopped

1/4 cup all-purpose flour

1 cup water

2 teaspoons Cajun seasoning

1/2 (21-ounce) package vegan shrimp

1/4 cup freshly squeezed lemon juice

1/2 teaspoon salt

1/4 teaspoon black pepper

4 cups cooked brown rice

1/2 cup chopped fresh parsley

1. In a large skillet over medium heat, add margarine and sauté onion, celery, carrot, garlic, and bell pepper until soft, about 5 minutes. Stir in flour to make a roux. Transfer vegetables to a 4-quart slow cooker.

2. Whisk in water, Cajun seasoning, vegan shrimp, lemon juice, salt, and black pepper. Cover and cook on low until vegetables are softened, about 4–5 hours.

3. Serve over brown rice and garnish with parsley.

Per Serving

Calories: 301 | Fat: 8g | Sodium: 527mg
Carbohydrates: 52g | Fiber: 5g
Sugar: 4g | Protein: 5g

CAJUN SEASONING

To make your own Cajun seasoning, use a blend of equal parts cayenne pepper, black pepper, paprika, garlic powder, onion powder, salt, and dried thyme.

Gumbo Z'herbes

SERVES 6

You won't miss the meat with all the delicious flavors in this gumbo. As they say in New Orleans, *"Laissez les bons temps rouler!"* Or, "Let the good times roll!"

Ingredients

½ cup olive oil

1 medium yellow onion, peeled and chopped

1 medium green bell pepper, stemmed, seeded, and chopped

2 medium stalks celery, trimmed and chopped

4 medium cloves garlic, peeled and minced

½ cup all-purpose flour

4 cups Vegetable Broth (see recipe in this chapter)

2 cups chopped okra

½ teaspoon dried thyme

½ teaspoon dried oregano

1 teaspoon salt

½ teaspoon black pepper

¼ teaspoon red pepper flakes

6 cups cooked brown rice

1. In a large skillet over medium heat, add oil and sauté onion, bell pepper, and celery on low heat until softened, about 4–5 minutes. Add garlic and sauté for 1 minute more.

2. Slowly whisk in flour to create a roux. Pour in Vegetable Broth and continue to whisk to remove all lumps.

3. Add all ingredients except rice to a slow cooker, and cook on high for 3–4 hours. Serve over cooked brown rice.

Per Serving

Calories: 443 | Fat: 19g | Sodium: 406mg
Carbohydrates: 60g | Fiber: 6g
Sugar: 2g | Protein: 7g

THE HOLY TRINITY
The base of some of New Orleans's most well-known dishes is referred to as the "holy trinity." It contains equal parts onions, bell pepper, and celery.

Thai Tom Kha Kai Coconut Soup
SERVES 4

In Thailand, this spicy soup is a full meal, served alongside a large plate of steamed brown rice, and the vegetables vary with the season and whim of the chef—broccoli, bell peppers, or mild chilies are common. Don't worry if you can't find lemongrass, as lime adds a similar flavor.

Ingredients

1 (14-ounce) can coconut milk

2 cups Vegetable Broth (see recipe in this chapter)

1 tablespoon soy sauce

3 medium cloves garlic, peeled and minced

5 large slices fresh ginger

1 stalk lemongrass, chopped

1 tablespoon freshly squeezed lime juice

2 small green chili peppers, seeded and chopped

1/2 teaspoon red pepper flakes

1 medium yellow onion, peeled and chopped

2 medium tomatoes, cored and chopped

1 medium carrot, peeled and thinly sliced

1/2 cup sliced mushrooms (any variety)

1/4 cup chopped fresh cilantro

1. In a large pot over low heat, combine coconut milk and Vegetable Broth. Add soy sauce, garlic, ginger, lemongrass, lime juice, chilies, and red pepper flakes. Heat, but do not boil.

2. When Vegetable Broth is hot, add onion, tomatoes, carrot, and mushrooms. Cover and cook on low heat until vegetables are softened, about 10–15 minutes.

3. Remove from heat and top with cilantro.

Per Serving

Calories: 253 | Fat: 20g | Sodium: 255mg
Carbohydrates: 16g | Fiber: 2g
Sugar: 6g | Protein: 5g

Korean-Style Hot Pot
SERVES 8

Serve this hot and spicy main dish with sides of steamed brown rice and kimchi (a mixture of fermented vegetables).

Ingredients

3 medium heads baby bok choy, cored and leaves separated

8 cups water

8 ounces cremini mushrooms, sliced

1 (16-ounce) package extra-firm tofu, drained and cubed

3 medium cloves garlic, peeled and thinly sliced

1/4 teaspoon sesame oil

1 tablespoon red pepper flakes

7 ounces enoki mushrooms

1. In a 4-quart slow cooker, combine whole bok choy leaves with water, cremini mushrooms, tofu, garlic, sesame oil, and red pepper flakes. Stir to mix well, then cover and cook on low for 8 hours.

2. Add enoki mushrooms and stir. Cook for an additional 30 minutes.

Per Serving

Calories: 98 | Fat: 3g | Sodium: 213mg
Carbohydrates: 11g | Fiber: 5g
Sugar: 5g | Protein: 11g

Posole

SERVES 6

This rich-tasting, spicy stew just needs a sprinkling of shredded red cabbage to finish it to perfection.

Ingredients

8 large dried New Mexican red chili peppers, stemmed and seeded (but reserve seeds)

6 cups Vegetable Broth (see recipe in this chapter), divided

3 medium cloves garlic, peeled and minced

2 tablespoons freshly squeezed lime juice

1 tablespoon ground cumin

1 tablespoon dried oregano

$2/3$ (10-ounce) package Gardein Meatless Chick'n Strips

$3/4$ cup all-purpose flour

1 teaspoon canola oil

1 large yellow onion, peeled and sliced

1 (40-ounce) can hominy

1. In a small, dry skillet over high heat, heat chilies until warmed through and fragrant, about 2–3 minutes. Do not burn or brown them.

2. In a medium pot over medium-high heat, combine chilies and reserved seeds with 4 cups Vegetable Broth, garlic, lime juice, cumin, and oregano. Bring to a boil and continue to boil for 20 minutes.

3. Meanwhile, in a sealable plastic bag, toss Chick'n Strips with flour to coat. In a large skillet over medium heat, add oil and brown chick'n on all sides, about 3 minutes.

4. Add onion and sauté until soft, about 5 minutes.

5. In a 4-quart slow cooker, combine remaining Vegetable Broth, hominy, and onion mixture.

6. Strain chili-stock mixture through a mesh sieve into the slow cooker insert, mashing down with a wooden spoon to press out the pulp and juice. Discard solids. Cook on low for 8 hours.

Per Serving

Calories: 295 | Fat: 6g | Sodium: 765mg
Carbohydrates: 49g | Fiber: 11g
Sugar: 6g | Protein: 12g

Curried Seitan Stew

SERVES 4

Adding a small amount of soy sauce to a curry dish gives it a richness that is normally achieved with fish sauce in recipes that aren't vegan.

Ingredients

2 tablespoons olive oil

1/2 medium yellow onion, peeled and chopped

2 medium cloves garlic, peeled and minced

1 teaspoon minced fresh ginger

2 tablespoons panang curry paste

1 teaspoon paprika

1 teaspoon granulated sugar

1/2 teaspoon cayenne pepper

1 teaspoon soy sauce

1 (14-ounce) can coconut milk

3 cups Vegetable Broth (see recipe in this chapter)

2 cups cubed traditional seitan

1/2 teaspoon salt

1/4 teaspoon black pepper

1/4 cup chopped fresh cilantro

1. In a 4-quart slow cooker, add all ingredients except cilantro. Cover and cook on low for 4 hours.

2. Garnish with cilantro before serving.

Per Serving

Calories: 413 | Fat: 27g | Sodium: 931mg
Carbohydrates: 20g | Fiber: 2g
Sugar: 4g | Protein: 24g

Succotash Stew

SERVES 6

Try adding chopped okra to this versatile southern stew.

Ingredients

1 pound dried lima beans

8 cups water, divided

2 (14-ounce) cans corn, drained

2 (14-ounce) cans diced tomatoes, undrained

2 bay leaves

1 teaspoon dried thyme

1 teaspoon dried oregano

1 teaspoon cayenne pepper

$\frac{1}{4}$ teaspoon salt

$\frac{1}{8}$ teaspoon black pepper

1. In a 4-quart slow cooker, combine beans and 7 cups water. Cover and cook on high for 4 hours. Drain beans and return to slow cooker.

2. Add remaining water, corn, tomatoes, bay leaves, thyme, oregano, cayenne pepper, salt, and black pepper. Cover and cook on low for 4 hours. Remove bay leaves before serving.

Per Serving

Calories: 300 | Fat: 1g | Sodium: 471mg
Carbohydrates: 57g | Fiber: 17g
Sugar: 10g | Protein: 17g

"Beef" and Barley Stew

SERVES 6

Classic and comforting, you can't go wrong with this spicy "beef" and barley stew on a cold night.

Ingredients

2 tablespoons olive oil

1 medium yellow onion, peeled and chopped

2 medium stalks celery, trimmed and chopped

1 medium carrot, peeled and chopped

1 medium green bell pepper, stemmed, seeded, and chopped

1 cup water

$2\frac{1}{2}$ cups tomato juice

$\frac{1}{3}$ cup uncooked barley

$1\frac{1}{2}$ teaspoons chili powder

$1\frac{1}{2}$ teaspoons dried parsley

2 bay leaves

4 veggie burgers, crumbled

$\frac{1}{8}$ teaspoon salt

$\frac{1}{8}$ teaspoon black pepper

1. In a large soup pot or stockpot over medium heat, add oil and sauté onion, celery, carrot, and bell pepper until almost soft, about 4–5 minutes.

2. Add water, tomato juice, and barley, stirring well to combine, then add chili powder, parsley, and bay leaves.

3. Reduce heat to low, cover, and cook for 20 minutes. Add veggie burgers and cook uncovered until barley is soft, about another 5 minutes.

4. Season with salt and black pepper; remove bay leaves before serving.

Per Serving

Calories: 197 | Fat: 7g | Sodium: 363mg
Carbohydrates: 23g | Fiber: 6g
Sugar: 5g | Protein: 10g

Black Bean and Butternut Squash Chili

SERVES 4

Squash is an excellent addition to plant-based chili in this hot and spicy southwestern-style dish.

Ingredients

2 tablespoons vegetable oil

1 medium yellow onion, peeled and chopped

3 medium cloves garlic, peeled and minced

1 medium butternut squash, peeled and chopped into chunks

2 (15-ounce) cans black beans, drained and rinsed

1 (28-ounce) can diced tomatoes, undrained

$3/4$ cup Vegetable Broth (see recipe in this chapter)

1 tablespoon chili powder

1 teaspoon ground cumin

$1/4$ teaspoon cayenne pepper

$1/2$ teaspoon salt

2 tablespoons chopped fresh cilantro

1. In a large stockpot over medium-high heat, add oil and sauté onion and garlic until soft, about 5 minutes.

2. Reduce heat to low and add remaining ingredients except cilantro.

3. Cover and simmer for 25 minutes. Uncover and simmer another 5 minutes. Top with fresh cilantro just before serving.

Per Serving

Calories: 366 | Fat: 8g | Sodium: 1,192mg
Carbohydrates: 60g | Fiber: 21g
Sugar: 9g | Protein: 16g

Pumpkin Chili
SERVES 6

Pumpkin is typically complemented by sugar, cinnamon, and other earthy spices, but you'll see that it's delicious with a dash of heat, like chili powder. Serve with sliced avocado on top.

Ingredients

2 tablespoons olive oil

1 medium yellow onion, peeled and diced

2 (14-ounce) cans diced tomatoes, undrained

1 cup Vegetable Broth (see recipe in this chapter)

1 medium pumpkin, rind and seeds removed, flesh cut into $\frac{1}{2}$" chunks

1 (14-ounce) can white beans (such as cannellini or Great Northern), drained and rinsed

2 tablespoons chili powder

3 teaspoons ground cumin

1 teaspoon salt

$\frac{1}{2}$ teaspoon black pepper

1. In a medium skillet, add oil and sauté onion on high for 3–5 minutes.

2. Transfer to a slow cooker, add remaining ingredients, and cook on low for 6 hours.

Per Serving

Calories: 205 | Fat: 5g | Sodium: 830mg
Carbohydrates: 33g | Fiber: 8g
Sugar: 8g | Protein: 8g

Black Bean, Corn, and Fresh Tomato Chili

SERVES 4

Tofutti makes a delicious nondairy sour cream called Sour Supreme, and it can be found in some national grocery store chains. Use it to garnish this deliciously spicy dish!

Ingredients

1 medium red onion, peeled and diced

1 medium jalapeño pepper, stemmed, seeded, and minced

3 medium cloves garlic, peeled and minced

1 (15-ounce) can black beans, drained and rinsed

1 (15-ounce) can corn, drained

3 tablespoons chili powder

1 tablespoon paprika

1 teaspoon dried oregano

1 teaspoon ground cumin

½ teaspoon chipotle chili powder

2 cups Vegetable Broth (see recipe in this chapter)

½ teaspoon salt

¼ teaspoon black pepper

2 cups diced tomatoes

¼ cup chopped fresh cilantro

4 tablespoons vegan sour cream

1. In a 4-quart slow cooker, combine all ingredients except tomatoes, cilantro, and sour cream. Cover and cook on low for 5 hours.

2. When the chili is done cooking, mix in tomatoes and garnish with cilantro. Top with vegan sour cream.

Per Serving

Calories: 234 | Fat: 5g | Sodium: 879mg
Carbohydrates: 43g | Fiber: 15g
Sugar: 7g | Protein: 11g

Chili con "Carne"

SERVES 4

Try BOCA Original Veggie Crumbles in this fast and fiery recipe as a plant-based alternative to ground beef.

Ingredients

1/2 cup diced white or yellow onion

1/2 cup diced green bell pepper

1 (12-ounce) package frozen veggie burger crumbles

2 medium cloves garlic, peeled and minced

1 (15-ounce) can kidney beans, drained and rinsed

2 cups Vegetable Broth (see recipe in this chapter)

1 tablespoon chili powder

1/2 tablespoon chipotle chili powder

1/2 tablespoon ground cumin

1 teaspoon dried thyme

1 tablespoon dried oregano

2 cups diced tomatoes

1 tablespoon tomato paste

1 tablespoon apple cider vinegar

1 teaspoon salt

In a 4-quart slow cooker, combine all ingredients. Cover and cook on low for 5 hours.

Per Serving

Calories: 248 | Fat: 5g | Sodium: 633mg
Carbohydrates: 31g | Fiber: 12g
Sugar: 5g | Protein: 23g

VEGAN BEEF

In addition to BOCA Original Veggie Crumbles, there are other types of plant-based ground beef on the market. Try Lightlife Gimme Lean Plant-Based Ground Beef, Hungry Planet Ground Beef, or TVP.

Cincinnati Chili

SERVES 4

Cincinnati chili is native to the state of Ohio and is typically served over spaghetti or on hot dogs. Serve with vegan cheese, additional chopped onions, and pinto beans as toppings, if desired.

Ingredients

1 medium yellow onion, peeled and chopped

1 (12-ounce) package frozen veggie burger crumbles

3 medium cloves garlic, peeled and minced

1 cup tomato sauce

1 cup water

2 tablespoons red wine vinegar

2 tablespoons chili powder

½ teaspoon ground cumin

½ teaspoon ground cinnamon

½ teaspoon paprika

½ teaspoon allspice

1 tablespoon brown sugar

1 tablespoon unsweetened cocoa powder

1 teaspoon hot sauce

1 (16-ounce) package whole-wheat spaghetti, cooked

1. In a 4-quart slow cooker, add all ingredients except spaghetti. Cover and cook on low for 5 hours.

2. Serve chili over cooked spaghetti.

Per Serving

Calories: 624 | Fat: 6g | Sodium: 812mg
Carbohydrates: 107g | Fiber: 13g
Sugar: 10g | Protein: 34g

WAYS TO SERVE
Cincinnati chili is known for being served up to five ways: Two-way means chili and spaghetti; three-way means chili, spaghetti, and vegan Cheddar cheese; four-way means chili, spaghetti, vegan cheese, and onions or pinto beans; and five-way means all of the above!

Fajita Chili
SERVES 6

Re-create the flavor of sizzling, spicy restaurant fajitas in your own home!

Ingredients

1 medium red onion, peeled and diced

1 medium jalapeño pepper, stemmed, seeded, and minced

3 medium cloves garlic, peeled and minced

1 (15-ounce) can black beans, drained and rinsed

1 (15-ounce) can diced tomatoes, drained

1 (7-ounce) package Gardein Meatless Chick'n Strips, cut into bite-sized pieces

2 cups Vegetable Broth (see recipe in this chapter)

2 teaspoons chili powder

1 teaspoon granulated sugar

1 teaspoon paprika

1/4 teaspoon garlic powder

1/4 teaspoon cayenne pepper

1/4 teaspoon ground cumin

1 teaspoon salt

1/4 teaspoon black pepper

In a 4-quart slow cooker, combine all ingredients. Cover and cook on low for 5 hours.

Per Serving

Calories: 147 | Fat: 3g | Sodium: 770mg
Carbohydrates: 21g | Fiber: 7g
Sugar: 4g | Protein: 11g

SIMPLIFY THIS RECIPE

One way to simplify this recipe is to use a packet of fajita seasoning (sold in the international aisle in many stores) in place of the chili powder, sugar, paprika, garlic powder, cayenne pepper, cumin, salt, and black pepper.

Lentil Chili

SERVES 6

Before using dried lentils in this spicy dish, rinse them well and pick through to remove any debris or undesirable pieces.

Ingredients

1 cup dried lentils

1 medium yellow onion, peeled and diced

3 medium cloves garlic, peeled and minced

4 cups Vegetable Broth (see recipe in this chapter)

¼ cup tomato paste

1 cup chopped carrots

1 cup chopped celery

1 (15-ounce) can diced tomatoes, drained

2 tablespoons chili powder

½ tablespoon paprika

1 teaspoon dried oregano

1 teaspoon ground cumin

1 teaspoon salt

¼ teaspoon black pepper

In a 4-quart slow cooker, add all ingredients. Cover and cook on low for 8 hours.

Per Serving

Calories: 176 | Fat: 1g | Sodium: 648mg
Carbohydrates: 33g | Fiber: 8g
Sugar: 6g | Protein: 10g

Red Hot Summer Chili
SERVES 8

This plant-based hot and spicy chili is full of summer vegetables, and you can add vegan chicken for a heartier dish.

Ingredients

1 medium bulb fennel, trimmed and diced

4 medium radishes, trimmed and diced

2 medium stalks celery, including leaves, diced

2 medium carrots, peeled and sliced into coins

1 medium yellow onion, peeled and diced

1 medium shallot, peeled and diced

4 medium cloves garlic, peeled and sliced

1 medium habanero chili pepper, stemmed, seeded, and diced

1 (15-ounce) can cannellini beans, drained and rinsed

1 (12-ounce) can tomato paste

$\frac{1}{2}$ teaspoon dried oregano

$\frac{1}{2}$ teaspoon black pepper

$\frac{1}{2}$ teaspoon dried rosemary

$\frac{1}{2}$ teaspoon cayenne pepper

$\frac{1}{2}$ teaspoon chipotle chili powder

1 teaspoon chili powder

1 teaspoon dried tarragon

$\frac{1}{4}$ teaspoon ground cumin

$\frac{1}{4}$ teaspoon celery seeds

2 medium zucchini, trimmed and cubed

10 medium Campari tomatoes, cored and quartered

1 cup corn kernels

1. In a 4-quart slow cooker, add fennel, radishes, celery, carrots, onion, shallot, garlic, habanero, beans, tomato paste, and all spices; stir. Cook on low for 6–7 hours.

2. Stir in the zucchini, tomatoes, and corn. Cook for an additional 30 minutes on high. Stir before serving.

Per Serving

Calories: 163 | Fat: 1g | Sodium: 503mg
Carbohydrates: 34g | Fiber: 9g
Sugar: 16g | Protein: 8g

CAMPARI TOMATOES

Campari is a variety of tomato that is grown on the vine and has a sweet, juicy taste. It is round and on the small side, but not as small as a cherry tomato.

Chapter Seven

MAIN DISHES

Hot and Spicy Garlic Pasta
SERVES 6

It's not fancy, but that's the beauty of this spicy recipe, which works for those times when you're too hungry to cook and just want to fill your stomach.

Ingredients

2 tablespoons olive oil

2 medium cloves garlic, peeled and minced

3 cups cooked whole-wheat pasta

2 tablespoons nutritional yeast

$\frac{1}{2}$ teaspoon dried parsley

2 tablespoons red pepper flakes

$\frac{1}{8}$ teaspoon salt

$\frac{1}{8}$ teaspoon black pepper

1. In a small skillet over medium-high heat, add oil and sauté garlic until almost browned, about 1–2 minutes. Transfer to a large bowl.

2. Toss garlic and olive oil with remaining ingredients.

Per Serving

Calories: 132 | Fat: 5g | Sodium: 52mg
Carbohydrates: 19g | Fiber: 3g
Sugar: 1g | Protein: 4g

REALLY HUNGRY? REALLY LAZY?
Garlic powder, fortified nutritional yeast, and salt is a delicious seasoning combination, and will give you a bit of a vitamin B_{12} perk-up. Use it over toast, veggies, popcorn, bagels, baked potatoes, and, of course, cooked whole-wheat pasta!

Artichoke and Olive Puttanesca

SERVES 6

Use fresh basil and parsley if you have it on hand, but otherwise, dried will taste fine in this delicious, spice-filled dish.

Ingredients

2 tablespoons olive oil

3 medium cloves garlic, peeled and minced

1 (14-ounce) can diced tomatoes, undrained

$1/4$ cup sliced black olives

$1/4$ cup sliced green olives

1 cup chopped artichoke hearts

2 tablespoons capers

$1 1/2$ teaspoons red pepper flakes

$1 1/2$ teaspoons chopped fresh basil

$2 1/4$ teaspoons chopped fresh parsley

$1/4$ teaspoon salt

1 (12-ounce) package whole-wheat pasta, cooked

1. In a large skillet over medium-high heat, add oil and sauté garlic until soft, 2–3 minutes. Reduce heat to low and add remaining ingredients except pasta.

2. Cook uncovered over low heat until most of the liquid from tomatoes is absorbed, about 10–12 minutes.

3. Toss with cooked pasta.

Per Serving

Calories: 258 | Fat: 6g | Sodium: 381mg
Carbohydrates: 44g | Fiber: 9g
Sugar: 3g | Protein: 9g

Sweet and Spicy Peanut Noodles
SERVES 4

Like a siren song, these noodles entice you with their sweet pineapple flavor, then scorch your tongue with fiery chilies. Very sneaky, indeed.

Ingredients

⅓ cup peanut butter

2 tablespoons soy sauce

⅔ cup pineapple juice

2 medium cloves garlic, peeled and minced

1 teaspoon grated fresh ginger

½ teaspoon salt

1 tablespoon olive oil

1 teaspoon sesame oil

3 small Thai (bird's eye) chili peppers, stemmed, seeded, and minced

¾ cup diced pineapple

1 (12-ounce) package brown rice noodles, cooked

1. In a small saucepan over low heat, stir together peanut butter, soy sauce, pineapple juice, garlic, ginger, and salt, just until well combined.

2. In a large skillet over medium heat, add olive oil and sesame oil and sauté chilies and pineapple, stirring frequently, until pineapple is lightly browned, about 2–3 minutes. Add noodles and sauté for another minute, stirring well.

3. Reduce heat to low and add peanut butter sauce mixture, stirring to combine well. Heat for 1 more minute until well combined.

Per Serving

Calories: 532 | Fat: 16g | Sodium: 888mg
Carbohydrates: 86g | Fiber: 4g
Sugar: 10g | Protein: 12g

Fusilli with Grilled Eggplant, Garlic, and Spicy Tomato Sauce

SERVES 4

Smoky, fruity flavors of grilled or roasted eggplant marry beautifully with tomatoes and garlic. Fusilli's deep crannies scoop up every drop of this spicy, complex sauce. Sprinkle with additional chopped parsley if desired.

Ingredients

1 (½-pound) eggplant, trimmed and cut lengthwise into 8 wedges

3 tablespoons olive oil, divided

⅛ teaspoon salt

⅛ teaspoon black pepper

3 medium cloves garlic, peeled and finely chopped

1 teaspoon red pepper flakes

½ cup roughly chopped fresh Italian parsley

4 cups tomato sauce

8 ounces whole-wheat fusilli pasta, cooked

1 tablespoon vegan margarine

¼ cup grated vegan Parmesan cheese

1. Heat grill, grill pan, or broiler. In a large bowl, toss eggplant wedges with 1 tablespoon olive oil; season with salt and black pepper. Grill or broil eggplant on the largest cut side for 4 minutes, until black marks show. Using tongs or a fork, turn to another side and grill 3 minutes more until it is bubbling with juices. Transfer to a cutting board to cool; cut into 1" pieces.

2. In a small bowl, mix remaining oil with garlic and red pepper flakes.

3. Heat a large skillet over medium-high heat. Add garlic mixture; allow to sizzle just 15 seconds, stirring with a wooden spoon, before adding parsley. Cook 30 seconds; add eggplant and tomato sauce. Bring to a simmer, then add cooked pasta and cook until heated through; remove from heat.

4. Finish by adding margarine and vegan cheese, adjusting for seasoning and tossing well to combine.

Per Serving

Calories: 403 | Fat: 14g | Sodium: 1,407mg
Carbohydrates: 63g | Fiber: 14g
Sugar: 15g | Protein: 12g

Baked Mexican Rice Casserole
SERVES 4

You can get this quick and spicy side dish into the oven in just a few minutes. It doesn't get easier to heat up a weeknight!

Ingredients

1 (15-ounce) can black beans, drained and rinsed

¾ cup salsa

2 teaspoons chili powder

1 teaspoon ground cumin

½ cup corn kernels

2 cups cooked brown rice

⅓ cup sliced black olives

½ cup grated vegan Cheddar cheese

1. Preheat oven to 350°F.

2. In a large pot over low heat, combine beans, salsa, chili powder, and cumin and warm through. Partially mash beans with a large fork.

3. Remove from heat and stir in corn and rice. Transfer to a casserole dish.

4. Top with sliced olives and vegan cheese. Bake for 20 minutes, or until cheese starts to brown.

Per Serving

Calories: 298 | Fat: 7g | Sodium: 900mg
Carbohydrates: 51g | Fiber: 12g
Sugar: 4g | Protein: 9g

IS YOUR SOY CHEESE VEGAN?
Many nondairy products do actually contain dairy, even if it says "nondairy" right there on the package! Nondairy creamer and soy cheeses are notorious for this. Look for casein or whey on the ingredients list, particularly if you suffer from dairy allergies, and if you're allergic to soy, look for nut- or rice-based vegan cheeses.

Creole Jambalaya
SERVES 8

Try Morningstar Farms Veggie Chik'n Strips and Tofurky sausage as an alternative to real meat in this hot and spicy pressure cooker recipe.

Ingredients

8 tablespoons vegan margarine

1 cup chopped onion

1 medium bell pepper, stemmed, seeded, and chopped

2 medium stalks celery, trimmed and chopped

3 medium cloves garlic, peeled and minced

3 cups Vegetable Broth (see recipe in Chapter 6)

1 cup water

1 (8-ounce) can tomato sauce

1 cup uncooked brown rice

2 bay leaves

2 teaspoons dried thyme

2 teaspoons cayenne pepper

2 teaspoons Cajun seasoning

$\frac{1}{8}$ teaspoon salt

1. In a pressure cooker over medium-low heat, melt margarine, then add onion, bell pepper, celery, and garlic. Cook until soft, about 15 minutes.

2. Add Vegetable Broth, water, tomato sauce, rice, bay leaves, thyme, cayenne pepper, and Cajun seasoning, then stir.

3. Lock the lid into place; bring to high pressure and maintain for 6 minutes. Remove from heat and allow pressure to release naturally.

4. Season with salt. Remove bay leaves before serving.

Per Serving

Calories: 156 | Fat: 5g | Sodium: 323mg
Carbohydrates: 24g | Fiber: 2g
Sugar: 3g | Protein: 3g

CREOLE CUISINE

Creole cuisine is similar to, but more refined than, Cajun cooking. Both use the "holy trinity" of onion, bell pepper, and celery as the base of many dishes. The cuisine hails from southern Louisiana but is influenced by Spanish, French, and African cuisines.

Spicy Southern Jambalaya
SERVES 6

Make this spicy and smoky Southern rice dish a main meal by adding some browned mock sausage or sautéed tofu. Garnish with chopped parsley if you like.

Ingredients

2 tablespoons olive oil

1 medium yellow onion, peeled and chopped

1 medium bell pepper (any color), stemmed, seeded, and chopped

1 medium stalk celery, trimmed and diced

1 (14-ounce) can diced tomatoes, undrained

3 cups Vegetable Broth (see recipe in Chapter 6)

2 cups uncooked brown rice

1 bay leaf

1 teaspoon paprika

½ teaspoon dried thyme

½ teaspoon dried oregano

½ teaspoon garlic powder

1 cup corn kernels

½ teaspoon hot sauce

1. In a large skillet or stockpot over medium-high heat, add oil and sauté onion, bell pepper, and celery until almost soft, about 3 minutes.

2. Reduce heat to low and add remaining ingredients except corn and hot sauce. Cover, bring to a low simmer, and cook for 45 minutes until rice is done, stirring occasionally.

3. Add corn and hot sauce and cook just until heated through, about 3 minutes.

Per Serving

Calories: 323 | Fat: 6g | Sodium: 147mg
Carbohydrates: 60g | Fiber: 5g
Sugar: 5g | Protein: 7g

GOT LEFTOVERS?
Heat up some refried beans and wrap up your leftover jambalaya in tortillas with some salsa and shredded lettuce to make plant-based burritos!

Bell Peppers Stuffed with Couscous
SERVES 4

Baked stuffed peppers are always a hit with those who appreciate presentation, and this spicy recipe takes very little effort.

Ingredients

4 cups Vegetable Broth
  (see recipe in Chapter 6)

3 cups uncooked couscous

2 tablespoons olive oil

2 tablespoons freshly squeezed
  lemon juice

1 cup frozen peas, thawed

2 medium scallions, trimmed
  and sliced

½ teaspoon ground cumin

½ teaspoon chili powder

4 medium green bell peppers,
  hollowed out and tops removed
  (but reserved)

1. Preheat oven to 350°F.

2. In a large saucepan over medium-high heat, bring Vegetable Broth to a boil. Add couscous. Cover, remove from heat, and let sit for 10–15 minutes, until couscous is cooked. Fluff with a fork.

3. Add oil, lemon juice, peas, scallions, cumin, and chili powder to couscous in saucepan. Stir to combine.

4. Stuff couscous into bell peppers and place the tops back on, using a toothpick to secure if needed.

5. Transfer to a baking dish and bake for 15 minutes, until peppers are tender.

Per Serving

Calories: 446 | Fat: 7g | Sodium: 68mg
Carbohydrates: 80g | Fiber: 8g
Sugar: 6g | Protein: 14g

Pumpkin and Lentil Curry
SERVES 3

Red lentils complement the pumpkin and coconut best in this salty-sweet curry, but any kind you have on hand will do. Look for frozen chopped squash to substitute for pumpkin to cut the preparation time. Serve over brown rice or other whole grains.

Ingredients

2 tablespoons olive oil

1 medium yellow onion, peeled and chopped

2 cups chopped pumpkin

1 tablespoon curry powder

1 teaspoon ground cumin

2 small red chili peppers, stemmed, seeded, and minced

2 whole cloves

3 cups Vegetable Broth (see recipe in Chapter 6)

1 cup dried lentils

2 medium tomatoes, cored and chopped

10 medium green beans, trimmed and chopped

3/4 cup canned coconut milk

1. In a large skillet over medium-high heat, add oil and sauté onion and pumpkin until onion is soft, about 5 minutes. Add curry powder, cumin, chilies, and cloves, and toast for 1 minute, stirring frequently.

2. Reduce heat to medium and add Vegetable Broth and lentils. Cover and cook, stirring occasionally, until lentils are tender, about 25 minutes.

3. Uncover and add tomatoes, green beans, and coconut milk, stirring well to combine. Heat uncovered just until tomatoes and beans are cooked, about 4–5 more minutes.

Per Serving

Calories: 463 | Fat: 21g | Sodium: 26mg
Carbohydrates: 53g | Fiber: 17g
Sugar: 12g | Protein: 19g

Black Bean Polenta Cakes
SERVES 4

All the flavors of the Southwest combine in this colorful confetti polenta loaf. Pan-fry individual slices if you like, or just enjoy it as it is. Serve with salsa, if desired.

Ingredients

1 (15-ounce) can black beans, drained and rinsed

6 cups water

2 cups cornmeal

1/2 medium red bell pepper, stemmed, seeded, and diced small

3/4 teaspoon ground cumin

1 teaspoon chili powder

1 teaspoon garlic powder

3/4 teaspoon dried oregano

1/2 teaspoon salt

1/2 teaspoon black pepper

2 tablespoons vegan margarine

1. Lightly grease a 9" × 5" loaf pan. Set aside.

2. In a small bowl, mash black beans with a fork until halfway mashed. Set aside.

3. In a large pot over medium-high heat, bring water to a boil, then slowly add cornmeal, stirring to combine.

4. Reduce heat to low and cook for 10 minutes, stirring frequently and scraping the bottom of the pot to prevent sticking and burning.

5. Add bell pepper, cumin, chili powder, garlic powder, oregano, salt, and black pepper. Stir well to combine. Continue to heat, stirring frequently, about 8–10 more minutes.

6. Add vegan margarine and stir well to combine, then add black beans, combining well.

7. Gently press into a prepared loaf pan, smoothing the top with the back of a spoon. Refrigerate until firm, at least 1 hour. Reheat in oven for 20 minutes at 375°F, slice, and serve.

Per Serving

Calories: 421 | Fat: 4g | Sodium: 595mg
Carbohydrates: 82g | Fiber: 11g
Sugar: 2g | Protein: 12g

New Orleans Red Beans
SERVES 8

This spicy, slow cooker dish is a New Orleans staple that is traditionally served on Mondays. Serve with steamed brown rice.

Ingredients

4 tablespoons vegan margarine

1 cup diced white or yellow onion

1 cup diced green bell pepper

1 cup diced celery

5 medium cloves garlic, peeled and minced

2 (15-ounce) cans red kidney beans, drained and rinsed

1½ cups water

4 teaspoons salt

2 teaspoons liquid smoke

1 teaspoon vegan Worcestershire sauce

2 teaspoons hot sauce

1 teaspoon dried thyme

2 teaspoons cayenne pepper

4 bay leaves

1. In a large skillet over high heat, add margarine and sauté onion, bell pepper, celery, and garlic until onion is soft, about 5 minutes.

2. Add all ingredients to a slow cooker. Cover and cook on low for about 6 hours.

3. Remove bay leaves before serving.

Per Serving

Calories: 125 | Fat: 3g | Sodium: 1,403mg
Carbohydrates: 19g | Fiber: 6g
Sugar: 2g | Protein: 6g

Indian-Spiced Chickpeas with Spinach (Chana Masala)

SERVES 3

This spicy recipe is enjoyable as is for a side dish or piled on top of brown rice or another grain for a main meal.

Ingredients

2 tablespoons vegan margarine

1 medium yellow onion, peeled and chopped

2 medium cloves garlic, peeled and minced

1 medium jalapeño pepper, stemmed, seeded, and minced

$^3/_4$ teaspoon coriander

1 teaspoon ground cumin

$^1/_2$ teaspoon cayenne pepper

1 (15-ounce) can chickpeas, undrained

3 medium tomatoes, cored and puréed

$^1/_2$ teaspoon curry powder

$^1/_4$ teaspoon turmeric

$^1/_4$ teaspoon salt

1 tablespoon freshly squeezed lemon juice

2 cups spinach, stems trimmed

1. In a large skillet over medium-high heat, add margarine and sauté onion, garlic, and jalapeño until almost soft, about 2 minutes.

2. Reduce heat to medium-low and add coriander, cumin, and cayenne pepper. Toast spices, stirring, for 1 minute.

3. Add chickpeas with liquid, tomatoes, curry powder, turmeric, and salt. Bring to a slow simmer. Allow to cook until most of the liquid has been absorbed, about 10–12 minutes, stirring occasionally, then add lemon juice.

4. Add spinach and stir to combine. Cook just until spinach begins to wilt, about 1 minute. Serve immediately.

Per Serving

Calories: 200 | Fat: 5g | Sodium: 452mg
Carbohydrates: 31g | Fiber: 9g
Sugar: 9g | Protein: 8g

Spicy Falafel Patties
SERVES 4

Health food stores sell a plant-based instant falafel mix, but it's not very much work at all to make your own from scratch. Add lettuce if desired.

Ingredients

1 (15-ounce) can chickpeas, well drained and rinsed

$\frac{1}{2}$ medium yellow onion, peeled and minced

1 tablespoon all-purpose flour

1 teaspoon ground cumin

$\frac{3}{4}$ teaspoon garlic powder

$\frac{3}{4}$ teaspoon salt

Egg replacer equivalent to 1 egg

$\frac{1}{4}$ cup chopped fresh parsley

2 tablespoons chopped fresh cilantro

4 medium pita bread pockets

$\frac{1}{4}$ medium tomato, cored and sliced

2 tablespoons Roasted Red Pepper Hummus (see recipe in Chapter 4)

1. Preheat oven to 375°F.

2. In a large bowl, mash chickpeas with a fork until coarsely mashed, or pulse in a food processor until chopped.

3. Add onion, flour, cumin, garlic powder, salt, and egg replacer, mashing together to combine. Add parsley and cilantro.

4. Shape mixture into 2" balls or 1"-thick patties. Place on a baking sheet and bake for 15 minutes or until crisp.

5. For each pocket, stuff falafel into a pita bread with some sliced tomatoes and top it off with Roasted Red Pepper Hummus.

Per Serving

Calories: 22 | Fat: 3g | Sodium: 787mg
Carbohydrates: 38g | Fiber: 6g
Sugar: 4g | Protein: 10g

Easy Pad Thai Noodles

SERVES 4

Volumes could be written about Thailand's national dish. It's sweet, sour, spicy, and salty all at once, and filled with as much texture and flavor as the streets of Bangkok themselves. Serve with bean sprouts, crushed toasted peanuts, extra chopped scallions, and lime wedges if desired.

Ingredients

1 pound thin brown rice noodles

¼ cup tahini

¼ cup ketchup

¼ cup soy sauce

2 tablespoons distilled white vinegar

3 tablespoons freshly squeezed lime juice

2 tablespoons granulated sugar

1 teaspoon red pepper flakes

¼ cup safflower oil

1 (16-ounce) package firm tofu, drained and diced small

3 medium cloves garlic, peeled and chopped

4 medium scallions, trimmed and chopped

½ teaspoon salt

1. In a large bowl, combine noodles with enough hot water to cover. Set aside to soak until soft, about 5 minutes.

2. In a small bowl, whisk together tahini, ketchup, soy sauce, vinegar, lime juice, sugar, and red pepper flakes.

3. In a large skillet over medium-high heat, add oil and sauté tofu and garlic until tofu is lightly golden brown, about 15 minutes. Add softened noodles, stirring to combine well, and sauté, about 2–3 minutes.

4. Reduce heat to medium and add tahini sauce mixture, stirring well to combine. Allow to cook for 3–4 minutes until well combined and heated through. Add scallions and salt and heat 1 more minute, stirring well.

Per Serving

Calories: 769 | Fat: 28g | Sodium: 1,359mg
Carbohydrates: 109g | Fiber: 7g
Sugar: 13g | Protein: 22g

TRULY THAI

Pad thai is supposed to be a bit greasy—which is why the noodles are fried in the oil. If you're not worried about fat and have quick-cooking thin rice noodles, you can omit the presoaking in water and just toss the noodles in with the tofu and garlic, and add extra oil.

Cajun-Spiced Cornmeal-Breaded Tofu

SERVES 3

Reminiscent of oven-fried breaded catfish, this is a spicy, southern-inspired breaded tofu. Bake as directed, or if you prefer, you can pan-fry in a bit of oil for 2–3 minutes on each side. Serve with hot sauce or barbecue sauce.

Ingredients

1 (16-ounce) package firm tofu, drained

2/3 cup unsweetened soy milk

2 tablespoons freshly squeezed lime juice

1/4 cup all-purpose flour

1/3 cup cornmeal

1 tablespoon Cajun seasoning

1 teaspoon onion powder

1/2 teaspoon cayenne pepper

1/2 teaspoon salt

1/2 teaspoon black pepper

1. Preheat oven to 375°F and lightly grease a baking pan with nonstick cooking spray.

2. Wrap drained tofu block in a clean kitchen towel. Place on a plate and weigh it down with a stack of plates or a heavy skillet. Allow to drain for 15 minutes.

3. In a wide, shallow bowl, combine soy milk and lime juice. In a separate bowl, combine flour, cornmeal, Cajun seasoning, onion powder, cayenne pepper, salt, and black pepper.

4. Slice tofu into triangles or rectangular strips and dip in soy milk and lime juice mixture. Next, coat well with cornmeal and flour mixture.

5. Transfer to prepared baking pan and bake for 8–10 minutes, until browned. Turn and bake the other side for 8–10 minutes.

Per Serving

Calories: 233 | Fat: 6g | Sodium: 673mg
Carbohydrates: 27g | Fiber: 3g
Sugar: 3g | Protein: 16g

Baked Mexican Tempeh Cakes

SERVES 4

Like tofu, tempeh can be baked in a flavorful sauce, but it does need to be simmered first, just to soften it up a bit. Serve topped with tomato salsa or hot sauce.

Ingredients

2 (8-ounce) packages tempeh

1 cup Vegetable Broth
(see recipe in Chapter 6)

$\frac{1}{3}$ cup tomato paste

3 medium cloves garlic, peeled
and minced

2 tablespoons soy sauce

2 tablespoons apple cider vinegar

3 tablespoons water

1$\frac{1}{2}$ teaspoons chili powder

$\frac{1}{2}$ teaspoon dried oregano

$\frac{1}{4}$ teaspoon cayenne pepper

1. If your tempeh is thicker than $\frac{3}{4}$", slice it in half through the middle to create 2 thinner halves. Then slice each block of tempeh into four fillets.

2. In a large skillet over medium-low heat, simmer tempeh in Vegetable Broth for 10 minutes. Drain well.

3. In a shallow dish, whisk together tomato paste, garlic, soy sauce, vinegar, water, chili powder, oregano, and cayenne pepper. Add tempeh, and allow to marinate refrigerated for at least 1 hour or overnight.

4. Preheat oven to 375°. Lightly grease a rimmed baking sheet or casserole dish with nonstick cooking spray.

5. Transfer tempeh to prepared baking sheet and baste with a bit of the marinade.

6. Bake for 15–17 minutes, until browned. Turn tempeh pieces over and baste with a bit more marinade. Bake another 15–17 minutes.

Per Serving

Calories: 250 | Fat: 11g | Sodium: 653mg
Carbohydrates: 17g | Fiber: 1g
Sugar: 3g | Protein: 23g

Chili and Curry–Baked Tofu

SERVES 3

If you like tofu and you like Indian- or Thai-style curries, you'll love this spicy baked tofu, with the taste of a slowly simmered curry in each bite. Use the extra marinade to dress a bowl of plain steamed brown rice.

Ingredients

1/3 cup coconut milk

1/2 teaspoon garlic powder

1 teaspoon ground cumin

1 teaspoon curry powder

1/2 teaspoon turmeric

3 small green chili peppers, stemmed, seeded, and minced

2 tablespoons maple syrup

1 (16-ounce) package firm tofu, drained and sliced into thin strips

1. In a shallow bowl, whisk together coconut milk, garlic powder, cumin, curry powder, turmeric, chilies, and maple syrup. Add tofu and marinate refrigerated for at least 1 hour, flipping once or twice to coat well.

2. Preheat oven to 425°F.

3. Transfer tofu to a casserole dish in a single layer, reserving marinade.

4. Bake for 8–10 minutes, until browned. Turn tofu over and spoon 1–2 tablespoons of marinade over the tofu. Bake 10–12 more minutes.

Per Serving

Calories: 216 | Fat: 11g | Sodium: 28mg
Carbohydrates: 18g | Fiber: 3g
Sugar: 11g | Protein: 14g

Cashew Seitan

SERVES 6

Hoisin is a soy-based, sweet and spicy sauce that is often used as a glaze for meats in Chinese dishes.

Ingredients

¼ cup rice wine

½ cup hoisin sauce

¼ cup soy sauce

½ cup water

1 tablespoon granulated sugar

2 (8-ounce) packages traditional seitan, cut into bite-sized pieces

2 tablespoons olive oil

1 medium red bell pepper, stemmed, seeded, and chopped

1 medium green bell pepper, stemmed, seeded, and chopped

4 medium cloves garlic, peeled and minced

½ cup cashew pieces

1. In a 4-quart slow cooker, combine rice wine, hoisin sauce, soy sauce, water, and sugar. Stir well, and then add all remaining ingredients except cashews.

2. Cover and cook on low for 6 hours. Garnish with cashew pieces before serving.

Per Serving

Calories: 260 | Fat: 10g | Sodium: 1,156mg
Carbohydrates: 25g | Fiber: 3g
Sugar: 11g | Protein: 17g

General Tso's Tofu

SERVES 2

The combination of sweet and spicy is what makes this plant-based dish a hit at Chinese restaurants across the country.

Ingredients

1 (16-ounce) package extra-firm tofu, drained

1 cup water

2 tablespoons cornstarch

2 medium cloves garlic, peeled and minced

1 teaspoon minced ginger

$\frac{1}{8}$ cup granulated sugar

2 tablespoons soy sauce

$\frac{1}{8}$ cup white wine vinegar

$\frac{1}{8}$ cup sherry

2 teaspoons cayenne pepper

2 tablespoons vegetable oil

2 cups chopped broccoli

1. Wrap drained tofu block in a clean kitchen towel. Place on a plate and weigh it down with a stack of plates or a heavy skillet. Allow to drain for 15 minutes. Chop tofu into cubes.

2. In a 4-quart slow cooker, combine all ingredients. Cover and cook on medium for 4 hours.

Per Serving

Calories: 414 | Fat: 23g | Sodium: 982mg
Carbohydrates: 33g | Fiber: 5g
Sugar: 16g | Protein: 23g

Seitan Barbecue "Meat"

SERVES 6

Sooner or later, all plant-based foodies discover the magically delicious combination of seitan and barbecue sauce in some variation of this classic favorite.

Ingredients

2 tablespoons vegetable oil

1 (8-ounce) package traditional seitan, sliced into thin strips

1 large yellow onion, peeled and chopped

3 medium cloves garlic, peeled and minced

1 cup Carolina Barbecue Sauce (see recipe in Chapter 2)

2 tablespoons water

1. In a large skillet over medium-high heat, add oil and sauté seitan, onion, and garlic until onion is just soft and seitan is lightly browned, about 5 minutes.

2. Reduce heat to medium-low and stir in Carolina Barbecue Sauce and water. Allow to simmer, stirring to coat seitan, until most of the liquid has been absorbed, about 10 minutes.

Per Serving

Calories: 167 | Fat: 7g | Sodium: 194mg
Carbohydrates: 18g | Fiber: 1g
Sugar: 13g | Protein: 7g

SEITAN SANDWICHES

Piled on top of sourdough along with some vegan mayonnaise, lettuce, and tomato, this recipe makes a perfect sandwich. Melt some vegan cheese for a simple Philly "cheesesteak"-style sandwich, or pile on the vegan Thousand Island dressing and sauerkraut for a seitan Reuben.

Hot and Spicy Black Bean Burgers
YIELDS 6 PATTIES

Veggie burgers are notorious for falling apart. If you're sick of crumbly burgers, try this simple method for making these hot and spicy black bean patties. It's 100 percent guaranteed to stick together.

Ingredients

1 (15-ounce) can black beans, drained and rinsed

3 tablespoons minced onion

1 teaspoon salt

1½ teaspoons garlic powder

2 teaspoons chopped fresh parsley

1½ teaspoons chili powder

⅔ cup all-purpose flour (or more if needed)

2 tablespoons vegetable oil

1 tablespoon hot sauce

1. In a blender or food processor, process black beans until halfway mashed, or mash with a fork. Transfer to a large bowl.

2. Add onion, salt, garlic powder, parsley, and chili powder, and mash to combine.

3. Add flour, a bit at a time, again mashing together to combine. You may need a little bit more or less than ⅔ cup. Beans should stick together completely. Form into 6 patties.

4. In a large skillet, add oil and pan-fry for 2–3 minutes on each side. Patties will appear to be done on the outside while still a bit mushy on the inside, so fry them a few minutes longer than you think they need. Top with hot sauce.

Per Patty

Calories: 161 | Fat: 5g | Sodium: 591mg
Carbohydrates: 24g | Fiber: 6g
Sugar: 0g | Protein: 6g

VEGGIE BURGER TIPS
Although this recipe is foolproof, if you have trouble with your veggie burgers crumbling, try adding egg replacer to bind the ingredients, then chill the mixture before forming into patties. Veggie burger patties can be grilled, baked, or pan-fried, but they do tend to dry out a bit in the oven. Not a problem; just smother with extra ketchup!

Indian Tofu Palak
SERVES 4

Palak paneer is a popular Indian dish of creamed spinach and soft cheese. This version uses tofu for a similarly spicy dish.

Ingredients

2 tablespoons olive oil

1 (16-ounce) package firm tofu, drained and cut into small cubes

3 medium cloves garlic, peeled and minced

2 tablespoons nutritional yeast

½ teaspoon onion powder

8 cups spinach, stems trimmed

3 tablespoons water

1 tablespoon curry powder

2 teaspoons ground cumin

½ teaspoon salt

½ cup plain soy yogurt

1. In a large skillet over low heat, add oil and sauté tofu and garlic. Add yeast and onion powder, stirring to coat tofu. Heat for 2–3 minutes, until tofu is lightly browned.

2. Add spinach, water, curry powder, cumin, and salt, stirring well to combine. Once spinach starts to wilt, add soy yogurt and heat just until spinach is fully wilted and soft, about 3 minutes.

Per Serving

Calories: 192 | Fat: 12g | Sodium: 361mg
Carbohydrates: 10g | Fiber: 4g
Sugar: 3g | Protein: 13g

Mexico City Protein Bowl
SERVES 1

This spicy dish is a quick meal for one in a bowl, reminiscent of Mexico City street food stalls, but healthier!

Ingredients

1 tablespoon olive oil

½ (16-ounce) package firm tofu, drained, pressed, and diced small

1 medium scallion, trimmed and chopped

½ cup peas

½ cup corn kernels

½ teaspoon chili powder

1 can black beans, drained and rinsed

2 (10") corn tortillas

1 teaspoon hot sauce

1. In a large skillet over medium-high heat, add oil and sauté tofu and scallion for 2–3 minutes. Add peas, corn, and chili powder. Cook another 1–2 minutes, stirring frequently.

2. Reduce heat to medium-low and add beans. Heat for 4–5 minutes, until well combined and heated through.

3. Place corn tortillas in the bottom of a bowl and spoon beans and tofu over the top. Season with hot sauce.

Per Serving

Calories: 890 | Fat: 25g | Sodium: 1,205mg
Carbohydrates: 121g | Fiber: 40g
Sugar: 12g | Protein: 53g

Orange-Glazed "Chicken" Tofu

SERVES 3

If you're missing Chinese restaurant–style orange-glazed chicken, try this easy tofu version. Double the sauce and add some veggies for a full meal over brown rice.

Ingredients

1 (16-ounce) package firm tofu, drained

$2/3$ cup orange juice

2 tablespoons soy sauce

2 tablespoons rice vinegar

1 tablespoon maple syrup

$1/2$ teaspoon red pepper flakes

2 tablespoons olive oil

3 medium cloves garlic, peeled and minced

$1\frac{1}{2}$ teaspoons cornstarch

2 tablespoons water

1. Wrap drained tofu block in a clean kitchen towel. Place on a plate and weigh it down with a stack of plates or a heavy skillet. Allow to drain for 15 minutes, then cut into ½"-thick triangles.

2. In a small bowl, whisk together orange juice, soy sauce, vinegar, maple syrup, and red pepper flakes. Set aside.

3. In a large skillet over medium heat, add oil and sauté tofu and garlic for just a few minutes, until tofu begins to brown.

4. Reduce heat to medium-low and add orange-juice mixture. Bring to a very low simmer and allow to cook, about 7–8 minutes.

5. In a small bowl, whisk together cornstarch and water until cornstarch is dissolved. Add to tofu mixture, stirring well to combine.

6. Bring to a simmer and heat for 3–4 minutes, until sauce thickens.

Per Serving

Calories: 243 | Fat: 15g | Sodium: 605mg
Carbohydrates: 16g | Fiber: 2g
Sugar: 10g | Protein: 14g

Saucy Kung Pao Tofu
SERVES 6

Try adding in a few more Asian ingredients to stretch this spicy recipe—bok choy, water chestnuts, or bamboo shoots, perhaps—and spoon on top of cooked noodles or steamed brown rice.

Ingredients

3 tablespoons soy sauce

2 tablespoons rice vinegar

1 tablespoon sesame oil

2 (16-ounce) packages firm tofu, drained and cubed

2 tablespoons vegetable oil

1 medium red bell pepper, stemmed, seeded, and chopped

1 medium green bell pepper, stemmed, seeded, and chopped

$2/3$ cup sliced button mushrooms

3 medium cloves garlic, peeled and minced

3 small green chili peppers, stemmed, seeded, and diced small

1 teaspoon red pepper flakes

1 teaspoon ground ginger

$1/2$ cup Vegetable Broth (see recipe in Chapter 6)

$1/2$ teaspoon granulated sugar

$1 1/2$ teaspoons cornstarch

2 medium scallions, trimmed and chopped

$1/2$ cup unsalted dry-roasted peanuts

1. In a shallow pan or zip-top bag, combine soy sauce, rice vinegar, and sesame oil. Add tofu and marinate refrigerated for at least 1 hour. Drain tofu, reserving marinade.

2. In a large skillet over medium-high heat, add vegetable oil and sauté bell peppers, mushrooms, garlic, chili peppers, and red pepper flakes until softened about 2–3 minutes. Then add tofu and heat until vegetables are almost soft, another 1–2 minutes.

3. Reduce heat to medium-low and add tofu marinade, ginger, Vegetable Broth, sugar, and cornstarch, whisking in the cornstarch to avoid lumps.

4. Heat 2 more minutes, stirring constantly, until sauce has almost thickened.

5. Add scallions and peanuts, and heat for 1 more minute.

Per Serving

Calories: 272 | Fat: 18g | Sodium: 462mg
Carbohydrates: 12g | Fiber: 4g
Sugar: 5g | Protein: 17g

Tempeh Jambalaya
SERVES 6

Unlike the famous New Orleans dish, this spicy jambalaya isn't meant to be brothy; instead, you'll cook the rice dish until all of the liquid is absorbed.

Ingredients

1 (13-ounce) package tempeh, cut into bite-sized squares

1 medium yellow onion, peeled and chopped

2 medium stalks celery, trimmed and chopped

1 medium green bell pepper, stemmed, seeded, and chopped

4 medium cloves garlic, peeled and minced

2 cups uncooked brown rice

2 teaspoons Better Than Bouillon No Chicken Base

5 cups water

1 (15-ounce) can tomato sauce

2 bay leaves

2 tablespoons Cajun seasoning

$1/4$ teaspoon dried thyme

2 teaspoons hot sauce

1 teaspoon salt

$1/4$ teaspoon black pepper

In a 4-quart slow cooker, combine all ingredients. Cover and cook on low for 6 hours, or until all of the liquid is absorbed.

Per Serving

Calories: 384 | Fat: 7g | Sodium: 1,284mg
Carbohydrates: 62g | Fiber: 4g
Sugar: 4g | Protein: 18g

BAY LEAVES

Bay leaves are often used to flavor soups, stews, and other liquids during cooking. They are typically dried and used whole, but you can also crumble them into a dish. Then you won't need to remove them before serving.

Spicy Chili-Basil Tofu

SERVES 3

This saucy stir-fry is a favorite in Thailand when made with chicken and fish sauce, but many restaurants offer a plant-based version with soy sauce and tofu instead. Serve with brown rice or rice noodles to sop up all the sauce.

Ingredients

2 tablespoons vegetable oil

4 medium cloves garlic, peeled and minced

5 small green chili peppers, stemmed, seeded, and diced

3 medium shallots, peeled and diced

1 (16-ounce) package firm tofu, drained and diced

$\frac{1}{4}$ cup soy sauce

1 tablespoon vegan oyster sauce

1 teaspoon granulated sugar

1 medium bunch Thai basil, stems trimmed

1. In a large skillet over medium-high heat, add oil and sauté garlic, chilies, and shallots until fragrant and browned, about 3–4 minutes.

2. Add tofu and heat for another 2–3 minutes, until tofu is just lightly golden brown.

3. Reduce heat to medium-low and add soy sauce, oyster sauce, and sugar, whisking to combine and dissolve sugar. Heat 2–3 more minutes, stirring frequently. Then add basil and heat, stirring 1 more minute, just until basil is wilted.

Per Serving

Calories: 263 | Fat: 15g | Sodium: 1,433mg
Carbohydrates: 19g | Fiber: 3g
Sugar: 10g | Protein: 16g

MAKE IT LAST

If tofu and chilies aren't enough for you, add some onions, mushrooms, or green bell peppers to fill out this dish. Or, for a bit of variety, try it with half basil and half fresh mint leaves.

Cajun Tempeh Po' Boy

SERVES 2

This hot and spicy recipe makes two very large sandwiches, so bring your appetite—or you can save some for later.

Ingredients

1 (13-ounce) package tempeh, cut into small, bite-sized squares

½ cup olive oil

5 medium cloves garlic, peeled and minced

1 medium yellow onion, peeled and chopped

2 teaspoons dried oregano

2 teaspoons dried thyme

2 teaspoons cayenne pepper

2 tablespoons paprika

1 teaspoon salt

¼ teaspoon black pepper

1 medium loaf French baguette, sliced crosswise and then lengthwise in half

2 cups shredded lettuce

2 medium tomatoes, cored and sliced

1. In a 4-quart slow cooker, combine all ingredients except bread, lettuce, and tomatoes. Cover and cook on high for 2 hours.

2. Assemble the sandwiches on bread by layering the tempeh, lettuce, and tomatoes.

Per Serving

Calories: 1,254 | Fat: 72g | Sodium: 1,950mg
Carbohydrates: 100g | Fiber: 8g
Sugar: 13g | Protein: 51g

ALL "DRESSED" UP

Traditional New Orleans po' boys are served either plain or dressed. Dressed means it's topped with lettuce, tomatoes, pickles, and mayonnaise, but you can substitute Vegenaise to keep the sandwich vegan.

"Short Rib" Tempeh

SERVES 4

No pigs necessary for this mouthwatering "rib" recipe!

Ingredients

1 (13-ounce) package tempeh, cut into strips

1 (28-ounce) can tomato sauce

$\frac{1}{2}$ cup water

2 tablespoons vegan Worcestershire sauce

2 tablespoons brown sugar

2 tablespoons dried parsley

1 teaspoon Tabasco sauce

$\frac{1}{4}$ teaspoon black pepper

$\frac{1}{4}$ cup freshly squeezed lemon juice

1 tablespoon soy sauce

In a 4-quart slow cooker, combine all ingredients. Cover and cook on low for 6 hours.

Per Serving

Calories: 265 | Fat: 9g | Sodium: 1,264mg
Carbohydrates: 29g | Fiber: 3g
Sugar: 15g | Protein: 20g

Thai Tofu-Coconut Curry

SERVES 6

Try this deliciously hot, easy curry tossed with rice noodles or over brown rice. You can find galangal root in Asian grocery stores.

Ingredients

1 (16-ounce) package extra-firm tofu, drained and sliced into $\frac{1}{2}$"-thick triangles

$\frac{1}{4}$ cup unsweetened shredded coconut

$\frac{1}{4}$ cup water

4 medium cloves garlic, peeled and minced

1 tablespoon minced fresh ginger

1 tablespoon minced galangal root

$\frac{1}{2}$ cup chopped onion

1 cup peeled and diced sweet potato

1 cup broccoli florets

1 cup snow peas

3 tablespoons tamari soy sauce

1 tablespoon vegan fish sauce

1 tablespoon chili-garlic sauce

$\frac{1}{2}$ cup minced fresh cilantro

$\frac{1}{2}$ cup canned light coconut milk

1. In a 4-quart slow cooker, combine tofu with coconut, water, garlic, ginger, galangal, onion, sweet potato, broccoli, snow peas, tamari, vegan fish sauce, and chili-garlic sauce.

2. Stir to distribute all ingredients evenly. Cook on low for 5 hours.

3. Stir in cilantro and coconut milk. Cook on low for an additional 20 minutes. Stir prior to serving.

Per Serving

Calories: 151 | Fat: 6g | Sodium: 767mg
Carbohydrates: 16g | Fiber: 4g
Sugar: 5g | Protein: 10g

Tofu Barbecue Sauce "Steaks"
SERVES 3

These spicy tofu "steaks" have a hearty texture and a meaty flavor. They are delicious as they are, or you can add them to a sandwich. If you've never cooked tofu before, this is a super easy, foolproof recipe to start with.

Ingredients

2 (16-ounce) packages firm tofu, drained

$\frac{1}{3}$ cup barbecue sauce

$\frac{1}{4}$ cup water

2 teaspoons balsamic vinegar

2 tablespoons soy sauce

2 tablespoons hot sauce

2 teaspoons granulated sugar

2 tablespoons olive oil

$\frac{1}{2}$ medium yellow onion, peeled and chopped

1. Wrap drained tofu block in a clean kitchen towel. Place on a plate and weigh it down with a stack of plates or a heavy skillet. Allow to drain for 15 minutes, then slice into $\frac{1}{4}$"-thick strips. Set aside.

2. In a small bowl, whisk together barbecue sauce, water, vinegar, soy sauce, hot sauce, and sugar until well combined. Set aside.

3. In a large skillet over medium-high heat, add oil and sauté onion until soft, about 5 minutes. Carefully add tofu. Fry tofu until lightly golden brown, about 2 minutes on each side.

4. Reduce heat to medium-low and add barbecue sauce mixture, stirring to coat tofu well. Cook until sauce absorbs and thickens, about 5–6 minutes.

Per Serving

Calories: 371 | Fat: 21g | Sodium: 1,256mg
Carbohydrates: 24g | Fiber: 3g
Sugar: 17g | Protein: 26g

TOFU VERSUS SEITAN

This recipe, like many pan-fried or stir-fried tofu recipes, will also work well with seitan, though seitan needs a bit longer to cook all the way through—otherwise it ends up tough and chewy.

Spicy Seitan Taco "Meat"

SERVES 6

Finely dice the seitan, or pulse it in the food processor until diced small, for maximum surface area and spice in this recipe, and pile up the taco fixings!

Ingredients

2 tablespoons vegetable oil

$\frac{1}{2}$ medium yellow onion, peeled and diced

$\frac{1}{2}$ medium red bell pepper, stemmed, seeded, and finely chopped

1 large tomato, cored and chopped

1 (8-ounce) package traditional seitan, finely chopped

1 tablespoon soy sauce

1 teaspoon hot sauce

2 teaspoons chili powder

$\frac{1}{2}$ teaspoon ground cumin

1. In a large skillet over medium-high heat, add oil and sauté onion, bell pepper, tomato, and seitan, stirring frequently, until seitan is browned and tomatoes and pepper are soft, about 5 minutes.

2. Reduce heat to medium-low and add soy sauce, hot sauce, chili powder, and cumin, stirring to coat well. Heat for 1 more minute.

Per Serving

Calories: 98 | Fat: 5g | Sodium: 312mg
Carbohydrates: 6g | Fiber: 2g
Sugar: 2g | Protein: 8g

Saag Tofu Aloo

SERVES 4

Saag Tofu Aloo is a fresh-tasting, protein-rich Indian dish that is only slightly spicy. *Saag* means "spinach" and *aloo* means "potato."

Ingredients

1 tablespoon canola oil

1 teaspoon cumin seeds

2 medium cloves garlic, peeled and minced

2 medium jalapeño peppers, stemmed, seeded, and minced

1 (16-ounce) package extra-firm tofu, drained and diced into $1/2$" cubes

$3/4$ pound red potatoes, peeled and diced

$1/2$ teaspoon ground ginger

$3/4$ teaspoon garam masala

1 (16-ounce) package frozen spinach

$1/4$ cup chopped fresh cilantro

1. In a large skillet over medium-high heat, add oil and sauté cumin seeds for 1 minute.

2. Add garlic and jalapeños. Sauté until fragrant, about 1 minute.

3. Add tofu and potatoes. Sauté for 3 minutes, then add ginger, garam masala, frozen spinach, and cilantro. Sauté for 1 minute.

4. Transfer to a 4-quart slow cooker. Cover and cook on low for 4 hours.

Per Serving

Calories: 226 | Fat: 8g | Sodium: 106mg
Carbohydrates: 26g | Fiber: 6g
Sugar: 3g | Protein: 16g

SERVING SUGGESTIONS

There are many different ways to enjoy Indian dishes such as this one. Try it over a bed of brown rice, scoop it up with naan (flatbread), or roll it up in chapati (another type of flatbread).

Spicy Tempeh Fajitas

SERVES 4

Add a dollop of vegan sour cream and salsa to finish off each of your fiery fajitas.

Ingredients

1½ (8-ounce) packages tempeh, cut into bite-sized pieces

2 medium cloves garlic, peeled and minced

1 teaspoon minced fresh ginger

¼ cup soy sauce

1 cup water

1 tablespoon olive oil

½ teaspoon chili powder

¼ teaspoon chipotle chili powder

¼ teaspoon black pepper

½ medium yellow onion, peeled and sliced

½ medium green bell pepper, stemmed, seeded, and sliced

1 medium jalapeño pepper, stemmed, seeded, and minced

½ cup sliced button mushrooms

8 (6") corn tortillas

1 medium tomato, cored and diced

¼ cup chopped fresh cilantro

1 medium lime, cut into wedges

1. In a 4-quart slow cooker, combine tempeh, garlic, ginger, soy sauce, water, oil, chili powder, chipotle chili powder, black pepper, onion, bell pepper, jalapeño, and mushrooms. Cover and cook on low for 6 hours.

2. Serve the fajitas on the tortillas and garnish with tomato, cilantro, and lime.

Per Serving

Calories: 310 | Fat: 12g | Sodium: 925mg
Carbohydrates: 31g | Fiber: 4g
Sugar: 3g | Protein: 21g

Simmered Coconut Curried Tofu

SERVES 3

Serve this spicy dish on top of rice or pasta. It's delicious either way!

Ingredients

1 tablespoon olive oil

1 (16-ounce) package firm tofu, drained and cubed

2 teaspoons sesame oil

3 tablespoons peanut butter

2 tablespoons soy sauce

2 tablespoons water

1 teaspoon curry powder

$\frac{1}{4}$ cup unsweetened coconut flakes

2 tablespoons minced fresh cilantro

1. In a large skillet over medium-high heat, add oil and sauté tofu until lightly golden brown, about 15 minutes.

2. Reduce heat to medium-low and add sesame oil, peanut butter, soy sauce, water, and curry powder, stirring well to combine. Heat, gently stirring, until tofu is tender, about 4–5 minutes.

3. Add coconut flakes and cilantro and heat just until well combined, about 1 more minute.

Per Serving

Calories: 321 | Fat: 25g | Sodium: 606mg
Carbohydrates: 9g | Fiber: 5g
Sugar: 3g | Protein: 18g

Tempeh Tamale Pie

SERVES 4

In a slight variation from the baked classic, this hot and spicy version of tamale pie features plump, moist cornmeal dumplings.

Ingredients

2 tablespoons olive oil

1 large yellow onion, peeled and minced

2 (8-ounce) packages tempeh, crumbled

1 medium jalapeño pepper, stemmed, seeded, and minced

2 medium cloves garlic, peeled and minced

1 (15-ounce) can diced tomatoes, undrained

1 (10-ounce) can diced tomatoes with green chilies, undrained

1 (15-ounce) can dark red kidney beans, drained and rinsed

4 canned chipotle peppers in adobo sauce, drained and minced

1/2 teaspoon Mexican chili powder

2/3 cup unsweetened soy milk

2 tablespoons canola oil

2 teaspoons baking powder

1/2 cup cornmeal

1/2 teaspoon salt

1. In a large skillet over medium heat, add olive oil and sauté onion, tempeh, jalapeño, and garlic for 5 minutes.

2. In a 4-quart slow cooker, combine tempeh mixture with tomatoes, tomatoes with green chilies, beans, chipotles, and chili powder. Cover and cook on low for 8 hours.

3. In a medium bowl, whisk together soy milk, canola oil, baking powder, cornmeal, and salt until well combined. Drop in 1/4-cup spoonfuls in a single layer on top of tempeh.

4. Cover and cook on high for 20 minutes without lifting the lid. The dumplings will look fluffy and light when fully cooked.

Per Serving

Calories: 582 | Fat: 25g | Sodium: 1,318mg
Carbohydrates: 58g | Fiber: 11g
Sugar: 8g | Protein: 31g

CANNED VERSUS FRESH TOMATOES

While fresh tomatoes are delicious, canned tomatoes are a better choice in some recipes because they have already been cooked. Skins and seeds have been removed from canned tomatoes, which is also a bonus when they might detract from the dish. There is also reason to believe that canned tomatoes are better sources of cancer-preventing lycopene simply because they are cooked.

Chapter Eight

SIDES

Moroccan Root Vegetables
SERVES 8

The Moroccan Root Vegetables recipe is good served with couscous and a vegan yogurt or side salad.

Ingredients

1 pound parsnips, peeled and diced

1 pound turnips, peeled and diced

2 medium yellow onions, peeled and chopped

1 pound carrots, peeled and diced

6 dried apricots, chopped

4 pitted prunes, chopped

1 teaspoon turmeric

1 teaspoon ground cumin

1/2 teaspoon ground ginger

1/2 teaspoon ground cinnamon

1/4 teaspoon cayenne pepper

1 tablespoon dried parsley

1 tablespoon dried cilantro

2 cups Vegetable Broth (see recipe in Chapter 6)

1 teaspoon salt

1. In a 4-quart slow cooker, combine parsnips, turnips, onions, carrots, apricots, prunes, turmeric, cumin, ginger, cinnamon, cayenne pepper, parsley, and cilantro.

2. Pour in Vegetable Broth and add salt.

3. Cover and cook on low for 9 hours, or until the vegetables are cooked through.

Per Serving

Calories: 108 | Fat: 0g | Sodium: 367mg
Carbohydrates: 26g | Fiber: 6g
Sugar: 12g | Protein: 2g

Saucy Vaishnava Veggies

SERVES 4

These simple, low-fat veggies will fill your kitchen with the smells and dreams of India as they simmer. Why not pick up a Bollywood movie to accompany your dinner?

Ingredients

1 (28-ounce) can diced tomatoes, undrained

2 large russet potatoes, finely chopped

$\frac{1}{2}$ teaspoon chili powder

2 teaspoons curry powder

$1\frac{1}{2}$ teaspoons ground cumin

$\frac{1}{2}$ teaspoon turmeric

1 medium head cauliflower, cored and chopped

1 medium carrot, peeled and diced

$\frac{3}{4}$ cup green peas

$\frac{3}{4}$ teaspoon red pepper flakes

$\frac{1}{4}$ teaspoon salt

1. In a large pot over medium heat, combine tomatoes, potatoes, chili powder, curry powder, cumin, and turmeric. Cover and cook for 10 minutes.

2. Add cauliflower, carrot, peas, and red pepper flakes and cook, covered, for 15 more minutes, until potatoes and vegetables are soft, stirring occasionally.

3. Season with salt.

Per Serving

Calories: 268 | Fat: 1g | Sodium: 582mg
Carbohydrates: 57g | Fiber: 11g
Sugar: 11g | Protein: 10g

INDIAN PLANT-BASED OPTIONS

In India, many vegetarians forswear eggs as well as onions and garlic for religious purposes, making Indian food an excellent choice for vegans. When eating at Indian restaurants, be sure to ask about ghee (clarified butter), which is a traditional ingredient, but oil is easily and frequently substituted for it.

Marinated Artichokes

SERVES 4

The Marinated Artichokes can be stored in the refrigerator for about 1 week, or about 2 months if you can them in a hot-water bath.

Ingredients

18 ounces fresh artichoke hearts

1/2 cup olive oil

1/4 cup apple cider vinegar

2 tablespoons freshly squeezed lemon juice

3 bay leaves

1 teaspoon dried oregano

1/2 teaspoon salt

1/2 teaspoon red pepper flakes

In a 2-quart slow cooker, combine all ingredients and stir well. Cover and cook on low for 2 hours.

Per Serving

Calories: 151 | Fat: 13g | Sodium: 685mg
Carbohydrates: 5g | Fiber: 2g
Sugar: 1g | Protein: 1g

Baby Bok Choy
SERVES 6

Dark, leafy bok choy is a highly nutritious vegetable that can be found in well-stocked groceries. Keep an eye out for light-green baby bok choy, which is a bit more tender but carries a similar flavor.

Ingredients

2 tablespoons soy sauce

2 tablespoons apple cider vinegar

2 tablespoons sesame oil

$\frac{1}{2}$ teaspoon garlic powder

1 teaspoon red pepper flakes

3 medium heads baby bok choy, cored and halved lengthwise

1. In a small bowl, whisk together all ingredients except bok choy.

2. In a 4-quart slow cooker, lay bok choy leaves and pour soy sauce mixture over them. Cover and cook on low for 3 hours.

Per Serving

Calories: 51 | Fat: 4g | Sodium: 329mg
Carbohydrates: 2g | Fiber: 1g
Sugar: 1g | Protein: 1g

Chipotle Corn on the Cob
SERVES 6

The corn husks resulting from this spicy recipe can be dried out and reused as a tamale casing. Garnish with extra chili powder and chopped cilantro.

Ingredients

6 medium ears corn, shucked

Water, as needed

3 tablespoons vegan margarine

$\frac{1}{2}$ teaspoon chipotle chili powder

$\frac{1}{2}$ teaspoon salt

1. In a 4-quart slow cooker, place corn and cover with water until it is 1" from the top of the slow cooker.

2. Cover and cook on high for 2 hours.

3. While corn is cooking, in a small bowl, combine margarine, chipotle powder, and salt. When corn is done cooking, drain and rub $1\frac{1}{2}$ teaspoons margarine mixture on each cob and then serve.

Per Serving

Calories: 122 | Fat: 4g | Sodium: 248mg
Carbohydrates: 22g | Fiber: 3g
Sugar: 5g | Protein: 4g

Cajun Collard Greens

SERVES 4

Like Brussels sprouts and kimchi, collard greens are one of those foods folks tend to either love or hate. They're highly nutritious, so hopefully this hot and spicy recipe will turn you into a lover if you're not already.

Ingredients

2 tablespoons olive oil

1 medium yellow onion, peeled and diced

3 medium cloves garlic, peeled and minced

1 pound collard greens, stems and ribs removed, leaves chopped

$3/4$ cup Vegetable Broth (see recipe in Chapter 6)

1 (14-ounce) can diced tomatoes, drained

$1\frac{1}{2}$ teaspoons Cajun seasoning

$1/2$ teaspoon hot sauce

$1/4$ teaspoon salt

1. In a large skillet over medium-high heat, add oil and sauté onion, garlic, and collard greens until onion is soft, about 5 minutes.

2. Add Vegetable Broth, tomatoes, and Cajun seasoning. Bring to a simmer, cover, and allow to cook until greens are soft, about 20 minutes, stirring occasionally.

3. Remove lid, stir in hot sauce and salt, and cook, uncovered, for another 1–2 minutes to allow excess moisture to evaporate.

Per Serving

Calories: 127 | Fat: 7g | Sodium: 650mg
Carbohydrates: 13g | Fiber: 6g
Sugar: 4g | Protein: 4g

HOW TO PREPARE COLLARDS
Give your collards a good rinse, then tear the leaves off the middle stem. Fold or roll all the leaves together, then run a knife through them to create thin strips, similar to a chiffonade cut used for herbs. The stems can be added to a vegetable broth or your compost pile.

Cilantro-Lime Corn on the Cob
SERVES 4

This pressure cooker Cilantro-Lime Corn on the Cob recipe couldn't be easier—or more delicious! To add a little more kick, increase the amount of cayenne pepper.

Ingredients

4 medium ears corn, shucked

$\frac{1}{2}$ cup water

2 tablespoons vegan margarine

2 tablespoons chopped fresh cilantro

2 teaspoons freshly squeezed lime juice

$\frac{1}{2}$ teaspoon salt

2 teaspoons cayenne pepper

1. Place the rack in the pressure cooker and place corn on rack. Pour in water.

2. Lock the lid into place and bring to low pressure; maintain pressure for 3 minutes. Remove the pressure cooker from heat, quick-release the pressure, and remove the lid.

3. In a small bowl, combine margarine, cilantro, lime juice, salt, and cayenne pepper until well blended.

4. When corn is cool enough to handle, spread $\frac{1}{4}$ of the mixture on each ear of corn.

Per Serving

Calories: 116 | Fat: 4g | Sodium: 348mg
Carbohydrates: 20g | Fiber: 2g
Sugar: 7g | Protein: 4g

Spicy Creamed Spinach

SERVES 6

You might not think that spinach would have much taste, but add red pepper flakes and your mouth will be telling a different story!

Ingredients

1 tablespoon vegan margarine

1 medium clove garlic, peeled and minced

1 tablespoon all-purpose flour

1 cup unsweetened soy milk

$\frac{1}{2}$ teaspoon salt

$\frac{1}{2}$ teaspoon red pepper flakes

$\frac{1}{4}$ teaspoon dried sage

1 (12-ounce) package frozen spinach, thawed

1. In a large skillet on high heat, melt margarine. Add garlic, and cook for 2 minutes before stirring in flour. Slowly pour in soy milk and whisk until all lumps are removed.

2. Add all ingredients to a 2-quart slow cooker. Stir, then cover and cook on low for 1–2 hours, until thickened.

Per Serving

Calories: 46 | Fat: 1g | Sodium: 268mg
Carbohydrates: 5g | Fiber: 2g
Sugar: 1g | Protein: 3g

VARIATIONS

You can simplify this recipe by going with a simple vegan margarine sauce that is flavored with salt, pepper, and sage, or make this savory dish even richer by adding a sprinkling of vegan cheese such as Daiya Mozzarella Style Shreds.

Spicy Turnip Greens

SERVES 4

In this spicy pressure cooker recipe be sure to use fresh or frozen turnip greens for best flavor and optimal nutrition.

Ingredients

1 tablespoon olive oil

½ medium yellow onion, peeled and diced

1 medium clove garlic, peeled and minced

1 teaspoon red pepper flakes

2 cups Vegetable Broth (see recipe in Chapter 6)

1 teaspoon Dijon mustard

1 pound turnip greens, stems and ribs removed, leaves chopped into large pieces

⅛ teaspoon salt

⅛ teaspoon black pepper

1. Bring pressure cooker to medium heat. Add oil, onion, garlic, and red pepper flakes. Cook until onion begins to soften, about 5 minutes. Add Vegetable Broth, mustard, and turnip greens; stir well.

2. Lock the lid into place and bring to high pressure; maintain for 5 minutes. Remove from heat and release pressure naturally. Add salt and black pepper.

Per Serving

Calories: 56 | Fat: 4g | Sodium: 130mg
Carbohydrates: 5g | Fiber: 2g
Sugar: 1g | Protein: 1g

Garlic and Gingered Green Beans
SERVES 4

This recipe doesn't use a lot of red pepper flakes, but a little can go a long way when it comes to taste!

Ingredients

1 pound green beans, trimmed and chopped

2 tablespoons olive oil

4 medium cloves garlic, peeled and minced

1 teaspoon fresh minced ginger

1 teaspoon red pepper flakes

$\frac{1}{8}$ teaspoon salt

$\frac{1}{8}$ teaspoon black pepper

1. Fill a large saucepan with water and set over high heat. Bring to a boil and cook green beans for just 3–4 minutes; do not overcook. Drain and rinse under cold water.

2. In a large skillet over medium-high heat, add oil and sauté garlic, ginger, green beans, and red pepper flakes. Cook, stirring frequently, until garlic is soft, about 3–4 minutes.

3. Season with salt and black pepper.

Per Serving

Calories: 98 | Fat: 7g | Sodium: 73mg
Carbohydrates: 9g | Fiber: 3g
Sugar: 2g | Protein: 2g

Warm Jicama Slaw

SERVES 6

Jicama is a crunchy root vegetable that is typically served cold but also works well in warm dishes because it retains its crunchy texture.

Ingredients

¼ cup freshly squeezed lime juice

¼ cup water

¼ cup orange juice

2 tablespoons vegetable oil

1 teaspoon apple cider vinegar

2 teaspoons red pepper flakes

2 cups peeled and shredded jicama

1 cup shredded cabbage

1 cup shredded carrots

1. In a small bowl, whisk together lime juice, water, orange juice, oil, vinegar, and red pepper flakes until well combined.

2. In a 4-quart slow cooker, combine jicama, cabbage, and carrots. Add lime juice mixture and stir. Cover and cook over low for 1 hour.

Per Serving

Calories: 73 | Fat: 4g | Sodium: 16mg
Carbohydrates: 8g | Fiber: 3g
Sugar: 3g | Protein: 1g

Maple-Glazed Roast Veggies
SERVES 4

These easy roast vegetables make an excellent spicy side dish. The vegetables can be roasted in advance and reheated with the glaze to save on time if needed. If parsnips are too earthy for you, substitute one large potato. Add tarragon to the sheet before roasting if you like.

Ingredients

3 medium carrots, peeled and chopped

2 small parsnips, peeled and chopped

2 medium sweet potatoes, peeled and chopped

2 tablespoons olive oil

$\frac{1}{8}$ teaspoon salt

$\frac{1}{8}$ teaspoon black pepper

$\frac{1}{3}$ cup maple syrup

2 tablespoons Dijon mustard

1 tablespoon balsamic vinegar

1 teaspoon hot sauce

1. Preheat oven to 400°F.

2. On a large baking sheet, spread out chopped carrots, parsnips, and sweet potatoes. Drizzle with olive oil and season with salt and pepper. Roast for 40 minutes, tossing once halfway through cooking time.

3. In a small bowl, whisk together maple syrup, mustard, vinegar, and hot sauce until combined.

4. Transfer the roasted vegetables to a large bowl and toss well with the maple syrup mixture.

Per Serving

Calories: 266 | Fat: 8g | Sodium: 360mg
Carbohydrates: 47g | Fiber: 6g
Sugar: 26g | Protein: 3g

SWEET AND SPICY GLAZE
This tangy and sweet glaze will lend itself well to a variety of roasted vegetables and combinations. Try it with roasted Brussels sprouts, beets, baby potatoes, butternut or acorn squash, or even with roasted turnips or daikon radish.

Potatoes Paprikash
SERVES 8

This spicy Hungarian classic is the perfect side dish to serve with a seitan roast.

Ingredients

1½ teaspoons olive oil

1 medium yellow onion, peeled, halved, and sliced

1 shallot, peeled and minced

4 medium cloves garlic, peeled and minced

½ teaspoon salt

½ teaspoon caraway seeds

¼ teaspoon black pepper

1 teaspoon cayenne pepper

3 tablespoons paprika

2 pounds red potatoes, thinly sliced

2 cups Vegetable Broth (see recipe in Chapter 6)

2 tablespoons tomato paste

½ cup vegan sour cream

1. In a large skillet over medium-high heat, add oil and sauté onion, shallot, and garlic until they begin to soften, about 1–2 minutes. Add salt, caraway seeds, black pepper, cayenne pepper, and paprika, and stir. Immediately remove from heat and transfer to a 4-quart slow cooker.

2. Add potatoes, Vegetable Broth, and tomato paste, and stir to coat the potatoes evenly.

3. Cover and cook on high for 2½ hours, or until the potatoes are tender.

4. Turn off the heat and stir in the vegan sour cream.

Per Serving

Calories: 133 | Fat: 4g | Sodium: 213mg
Carbohydrates: 24g | Fiber: 4g
Sugar: 3g | Protein: 3g

Lime-Soaked Poblanos

SERVES 4

Simple and fresh, this easy recipe can be used as the filling for tacos or burritos, or as a topping on a nopalitos (cactus) salad.

Ingredients

$\frac{1}{4}$ cup freshly squeezed lime juice

$\frac{1}{4}$ cup water

2 medium cloves garlic, peeled and minced

2 tablespoons chopped fresh cilantro

$\frac{1}{2}$ teaspoon salt

4 medium poblano chili peppers, stemmed, seeded, and sliced

In a 4-quart slow cooker, combine all ingredients and stir until well combined. Cover and cook on low for 4 hours.

Per Serving

Calories: 56 | Fat: 1g | Sodium: 299mg
Carbohydrates: 11g | Fiber: 4g
Sugar: 0g | Protein: 2g

Spicy Chipotle and Thyme Mashed Sweet Potatoes

SERVES 6

To substitute fresh thyme for dried thyme in this spicy pressure cooker recipe, use $^1/_2$ tablespoon of the fresh herb.

Ingredients

2 cups water

6 cups cubed sweet potatoes

4 tablespoons vegan margarine

3 medium cloves garlic, peeled and minced

$^1/_2$ teaspoon dried chipotle pepper

$^1/_2$ teaspoon dried thyme

$^1/_8$ teaspoon salt

$^1/_8$ teaspoon black pepper

1. Pour water into the pressure cooker and add sweet potatoes. Lock the lid into place and bring to high pressure. Once achieved, turn the heat to low and cook for 5 minutes. Remove from heat and release pressure naturally.

2. Drain potatoes into a colander. Add margarine to the pressure cooker and sauté garlic for about 2 minutes. Remove the pressure cooker from the heat. Add sweet potatoes, chipotle pepper, and thyme. Mash the potatoes using a potato masher or electric mixer. Season with salt and black pepper.

Per Serving

Calories: 284 | Fat: 3g | Sodium: 191mg
Carbohydrates: 59g | Fiber: 8g
Sugar: 19g | Protein: 5g

Spicy Summer Squash Sauté
SERVES 2

Green zucchinis and yellow summer squash absorb the spicy flavors in this recipe like magic, though little enhancement is needed with their fresh, natural flavor. Toss these veggies with some cooked whole-wheat orzo or linguine to make it a main dish.

Ingredients

2 tablespoons olive oil

1 medium yellow onion, peeled and chopped

2 medium cloves garlic, peeled and minced

2 medium zucchini, trimmed and sliced into coins

2 medium summer squash, sliced thin

1 large tomato, cored and diced

2 teaspoons Italian seasoning

1 tablespoon nutritional yeast

2 teaspoons hot sauce

1. In a large skillet over medium-high heat, add oil and sauté onion and garlic for 1–2 minutes, then add zucchini, summer squash, and tomato. Heat, stirring frequently, until squash is soft, about 4–5 minutes.

2. Season with Italian seasoning and heat for 1 more minute.

3. Stir in nutritional yeast and hot sauce.

Per Serving

Calories: 232 | Fat: 14g | Sodium: 182mg
Carbohydrates: 23g | Fiber: 7g
Sugar: 14g | Protein: 7g

Potato and Veggie Fritters
SERVES 3

These easy potato fritters are similar to an Indian snack called bhaji. To get the idea, add a few shakes of some Indian spices: curry, turmeric, or garam masala. Garnish with chopped cilantro and serve with mint chutney for dipping.

Ingredients

3 medium russet potatoes, peeled

1/4 cup unsweetened soy milk

1/4 cup whole-wheat flour

1/2 teaspoon garlic powder

1/2 teaspoon onion powder

1/2 teaspoon chili powder

1/2 teaspoon ground cumin

1/2 teaspoon cayenne pepper

1/2 cup frozen peas, corn, and diced carrots mix

1/8 teaspoon salt

1/8 teaspoon black pepper

2 tablespoons vegetable oil

1. In a large saucepan over medium-high heat, combine potatoes with enough water to cover. Bring to a boil and cook until potatoes are tender, about 20 minutes. Drain and allow to cool.

2. Mash potatoes together with soy milk, flour, garlic powder, onion powder, chili powder, cumin, cayenne pepper, frozen vegetables, salt, and black pepper until mixture is thick and potatoes are well mashed, adding a little more soy milk or flour as needed. Mixture should be dry but sticky.

3. Form into 2" patties in a large skillet over medium heat, add oil and fry patties for 3–4 minutes on each side or until browned and crispy.

Per Serving

Calories: 293 | Fat: 9g | Sodium: 138mg
Carbohydrates: 46g | Fiber: 6g
Sugar: 3g | Protein: 6g

Maple Baked Beans

SERVES 12

Tailor these saucy, spicy Boston-style baked beans to your liking by adding extra molasses or some TVP crumbles for a meaty texture.

Ingredients

3 cups dried pinto beans

9 cups water

1 medium yellow onion, peeled and chopped

$2/3$ cup maple syrup

$1/4$ cup Carolina Barbecue Sauce (see recipe in Chapter 2)

2 tablespoons molasses

1 tablespoon Dijon mustard

1 tablespoon chili powder

1 tablespoon cayenne pepper

1 teaspoon paprika

$1\frac{1}{2}$ teaspoons salt

$3/4$ teaspoon black pepper

1. In a large saucepan or bowl, combine beans in water to cover and allow to soak at least 8 hours or overnight.

2. Preheat oven to 350°F.

3. Drain beans. In a large ovenproof pot or Dutch oven over medium-high heat, combine beans and remaining ingredients. Bring to a rolling boil on the stove.

4. Cover and transfer beans to oven. Bake for $1\frac{1}{2}$ hours, stirring once or twice. Uncover and cook 1 more hour.

5. Alternatively, beans can be simmered over low heat on the stovetop for $1\frac{1}{2}$–2 hours.

Per Serving

Calories: 258 | Fat: 2g | Sodium: 356mg
Carbohydrates: 51g | Fiber: 12g
Sugar: 16g | Protein: 12g

Spanish Rice

SERVES 8

Cooking rice in tomatoes, chili powder, and bell pepper is the key to this slow cooker Spanish Rice.

Ingredients

2 cups uncooked brown rice

2 tablespoons vegan margarine

2 cups water

2 cups Vegetable Broth
(see recipe in Chapter 6)

1 medium yellow onion, peeled
and diced

1 medium green bell pepper, stemmed,
seeded, and diced

1 cup diced canned tomatoes,
undrained

2 tablespoons diced pickled jalapeño
peppers

1 teaspoon chili powder

½ teaspoon garlic powder

1 teaspoon salt

¼ teaspoon black pepper

In a 4-quart slow cooker, combine all ingredients. Cover and cook on low for 4–5 hours, until rice is soft.

Per Serving

Calories: 248 | Fat: 3g | Sodium: 401mg
Carbohydrates: 50g | Fiber: 5g
Sugar: 2g | Protein: 5g

Kimchi-Style Cabbage

YIELDS 4 CUPS

If you can't find Korean chili powder to use in this pressure cooker dish, substitute plain chili powder, which is also made from crushed red peppers.

Ingredients

1 medium clove garlic, peeled and minced

1 teaspoon fresh ginger, minced

6 medium scallions, trimmed and sliced

$\frac{1}{2}$ cup water

$\frac{1}{4}$ cup soy sauce

1 tablespoon Korean chili powder

4 cups chopped (2" pieces) Napa cabbage

1 cup julienned carrots

In a pressure cooker, combine garlic, ginger, scallions, water, soy sauce, and chili powder; stir well. Add cabbage and carrots. Lock on the lid. Bring to high pressure; maintain pressure for 2 minutes. Remove the pan from the heat, quick-release the pressure, and remove the lid.

Per 1 Cup

Calories: 50 | Fat: 0g | Sodium: 967mg
Carbohydrates: 10g | Fiber: 4g
Sugar: 4g | Protein: 3g

KIMCHI

Kimchi is a popular Korean condiment that is often used as the base for other recipes. Traditional recipes call for fermenting the mixture until pickled, but you can make "kimchi-style" cabbage by pressure-cooking the ingredients instead of fermenting.

Kale with Crushed Red Pepper
SERVES 4

The antioxidant-rich dark leafy greens found in this spicy dish are nutritional powerhouses loaded with calcium, beta carotene, and vitamin C. They're also high in fiber and phytochemicals. Serve this plant-based dish sprinkled with grated vegan Parmesan cheese if desired.

Ingredients

2 teaspoons plus ⅛ teaspoon salt, divided

2 pounds kale, stems and ribs removed

1 tablespoon olive oil

1 medium red onion, peeled and chopped

1 tablespoon chopped garlic

2 tablespoons red pepper flakes

2 teaspoons chopped fresh thyme leaves

¼ cup dry sherry

⅛ teaspoon black pepper

1. Fill a large pot with water and set over medium-high heat. Bring to a rolling boil, then add 2 teaspoons salt and kale and cook for 10 minutes, until it has lost its waxy coating and the leaves are tender. Transfer to a colander to drain, reserving about ½ cup cooking liquid. Roughly chop the kale.

2. In a large skillet over medium heat, add oil and sauté onion, garlic, red pepper flakes, and thyme. Cook over medium heat until onion is soft and starting to brown around the edges, about 6 minutes. Add sherry; cook until all alcohol has evaporated, about 5 minutes. Add kale; cook 10 minutes more. Season with remaining salt and black pepper.

Per Serving

Calories: 98 | Fat: 4g | Sodium: 588mg
Carbohydrates: 14g | Fiber: 4g
Sugar: 4g | Protein: 4g

Szechuan Stir-Fried Cabbage with Hot Peppers

SERVES 5

The spices in this Chinese cabbage dish are so delectable that they can make you forget about anything and everything else!

Ingredients

1/4 cup plus 2 tablespoons peanut oil, divided

8 dried red chili peppers, seeded and quartered

1 (1") piece fresh ginger, peeled and finely chopped

1 medium head cabbage (preferably Chinese cabbage, but any variety is okay), cored and chopped into 2" pieces

1/2 teaspoon cornstarch

1 tablespoon soy sauce

1 teaspoon dry sherry

1 teaspoon granulated sugar

1 teaspoon rice vinegar

1 teaspoon Asian sesame oil

1. In a wok or skillet over high heat, heat 1/4 cup oil. Stir in the peppers and fry, stirring, for 1 minute, until the peppers darken in color. Transfer peppers and oil to a bowl and set aside.

2. Pour remaining oil into wok; add ginger and cook for a few seconds, until fragrant. Add the cabbage all at once. Fry, stirring, for 1 minute.

3. In a small bowl, combine cornstarch, soy sauce, and sherry. Add to wok. Stir until cornstarch cooks and forms a thick sauce, about 5 minutes; add sugar and vinegar. Sprinkle in sesame oil and pour in red peppers and their oil. Stir to combine well.

Per Serving

Calories: 207 | Fat: 17g | Sodium: 291mg
Carbohydrates: 11g | Fiber: 3g
Sugar: 7g | Protein: 4g

Spiced "Baked" Eggplant

SERVES 4

Serve this slow cooker Spiced "Baked" Eggplant as a main dish over brown rice or as a side dish as is.

Ingredients

1 pound eggplant, trimmed and cubed

$\frac{1}{3}$ cup sliced yellow onion

2 teaspoons red pepper flakes

$\frac{1}{2}$ teaspoon dried rosemary

$\frac{1}{4}$ cup freshly squeezed lemon juice

In a 2-quart slow cooker, combine all ingredients. Cover and cook on low for 3 hours, or until eggplant is tender.

Per Serving

Calories: 41 | Fat: 0g | Sodium: 2mg
Carbohydrates: 10g | Fiber: 4g
Sugar: 6g | Protein: 2g

COLD SNAP

Take care not to put a cold ceramic insert directly into the slow cooker. The sudden shift in temperature can cause it to crack. If you want to prepare your ingredients the night before use, refrigerate them in reusable containers, not in the insert.

Baked Sweet Potato Fries

SERVES 3

Brown sugar adds a sweet touch to these yummy sweet potato fries. If you like your fries with even more of a kick, add some red pepper flakes to the mix. Garnish with red pepper flakes and chopped parsley if you like.

Ingredients

2 large sweet potatoes, peeled and sliced into fries

2 tablespoons olive oil

1/4 teaspoon garlic powder

1/2 teaspoon paprika

1/2 teaspoon brown sugar

1/2 teaspoon chili powder

1/4 teaspoon sea salt

1/2 teaspoon cayenne pepper

1. Preheat oven to 400°F.

2. Spread sweet potatoes on a large baking sheet and drizzle with olive oil, tossing gently to coat.

3. In a small bowl, combine remaining ingredients. Sprinkle over potatoes, coating evenly and tossing as needed.

4. Bake for 10 minutes, turning once. Taste, and sprinkle with a bit more sea salt if needed.

Per Serving

Calories: 193 | Fat: 9g | Sodium: 185mg
Carbohydrates: 26g | Fiber: 4g
Sugar: 9g | Protein: 3g

Spicy Okra and Tomatoes

SERVES 4

Generally, people either love okra or hate it—there's almost no in-between. Native to Africa and used in southern United States cooking, okra pods add unique color and texture to the dinner table. Look for pods that are uniform in color, without any dark or soft spots.

Ingredients

1½ pounds okra, cut into 1" pieces

1⅛ teaspoons salt, divided

2 tablespoons vegetable oil

2 medium yellow onions, thinly sliced

½ teaspoon finely minced fresh ginger

2 medium tomatoes, cored, seeded, and roughly chopped

2 Thai (bird's eye) chili peppers, stemmed, seeded, and finely chopped

2 medium cloves garlic, peeled and finely minced

⅛ teaspoon black pepper

1. Fill a medium saucepan with water and set over medium-high heat. Bring to a boil. Add okra and 1 teaspoon salt, reduce heat to medium-low, and let simmer until okra is tender, about 3–4 minutes. Drain okra and set aside.

2. In a large skillet over high heat, add oil and sauté onions, ginger, tomatoes, and chilies until onions are soft and fragrant, about 5 minutes.

3. Reduce the heat to medium, add garlic, and sauté until garlic is soft, another 3–4 minutes.

4. Add okra, remaining salt, and black pepper. Cook until okra is just heated through, about 2–3 minutes.

Per Serving

Calories: 143 | Fat: 7g | Sodium: 489mg
Carbohydrates: 18g | Fiber: 6g
Sugar: 9g | Protein: 5g

WHAT MAKES OKRA SLIMY?
One of the reasons people are turned off by okra is because it has a natural slime. (There's no polite way to put it.) Okra is part of the mallow family, a group of plants that exude a gelatinous substance when cut. The slime is perfectly edible and, some might say, pleasant. Give it a try—you might even come to like it.

Spicy Dill Pickles
YIELDS 48 PICKLES

A hotter take on the classic American dill pickle. Feel free to turn up the heat as you like.

Ingredients

12 pickling cucumbers (also called Kirbys), cut lengthwise into quarters

2 medium serrano chili peppers, stemmed, seeded, and thinly sliced

2 cups distilled white vinegar

1½ cups water

1 tablespoon coriander seeds

1 tablespoon peppercorns

1 teaspoon fennel seeds

1 teaspoon red pepper flakes

1 medium bunch fresh dill, roughly chopped

1. In a large bowl, combine all ingredients except dill. Stir and let sit at room temperature for at least 2 hours.

2. Divide dill evenly between two or three jars. Divide cucumber spears evenly between jars as well.

3. Pour pickling liquid over cucumber spears.

4. Screw lids on and store refrigerated for 2 days before using. Enjoy these Spicy Dill Pickles within a week.

Per Pickle

Calories: 7 | Fat: 0g | Sodium: 1mg
Carbohydrates: 2g | Fiber: 0g
Sugar: 1g | Protein: 0g

Rum Chilies

YIELDS ABOUT 2 CUPS PICKLES

Try these on top of vegan fish for a little spicy Caribbean flair. Be sure to use gloves when handling the extremely spicy Scotch bonnet chilies. If you can't find them, you can substitute habanero chili peppers.

Ingredients

1 tablespoon granulated sugar

1 cup apple cider vinegar

2 bay leaves

1 teaspoon coriander seeds

1 teaspoon mustard seeds

1 medium red onion, peeled and thinly sliced

4 medium cloves garlic, peeled and thinly sliced

4 medium Scotch bonnet chili peppers, stemmed, seeded, and ribs removed, thinly sliced horizontally

4 medium jalapeño peppers, stemmed, seeded, and thinly sliced

2 small carrots, peeled and thinly sliced

2 cups dark rum

1. In a large nonreactive saucepan over medium-high heat, combine sugar, vinegar, bay leaves, coriander seeds, and mustard seeds. Bring to a boil, then reduce heat to low and let simmer for 5 minutes. Remove from heat and let cool.

2. In a large, clean glass preserving jar or several smaller ones, combine onion, garlic, peppers, and carrots.

3. When the vinegar mixture has cooled to lukewarm, add rum. Stir to combine, then pour mixture into jars.

4. Screw lids on jars and store refrigerated for a few days before using. Enjoy within a week.

Per 1 Cup

Calories: 143 | Fat: 1g | Sodium: 45mg
Carbohydrates: 21g | Fiber: 5g
Sugar: 11g | Protein: 3g

PRESERVING IN ALCOHOL

Besides salt and vinegar, you can also preserve or "pickle" chilies in alcohol. Using alcohol is one of the simplest methods of preserving because it kills bacteria. Alcohols like rum have a high sugar content, so they will give the chili peppers sweetness as well. Try pickling with vodka, gin, tequila, or even whiskey.

Spicy Chowchow

YIELDS 8 CUPS

This sweet and spicy relish is a southern favorite. Try it alongside a meal with mashed potatoes. For less heat, remove the seeds and ribs from the jalapeño peppers.

Ingredients

½ medium head green cabbage, cored and thinly shredded

10 medium jalapeño peppers, stemmed but seeds and ribs reserved, finely chopped

3 medium red bell peppers, stemmed, seeded, and chopped

3 medium green bell peppers, stemmed, seeded, and chopped

3 medium green tomatoes, cored and chopped

2 medium sweet onions, peeled and chopped

⅓ cup salt

2 cups apple cider vinegar

1 cup granulated sugar

2 teaspoons celery seeds

2 teaspoons fennel seeds

2 teaspoons mustard seeds

2 teaspoons turmeric

1. In a large bowl, combine cabbage, jalapeños, bell peppers, tomatoes, and onions. Add the salt and stir well to combine. Cover and refrigerate for 6–8 hours, then rinse and drain well in a colander.

2. In a large pot over medium-high heat, combine vegetables with vinegar, sugar, celery seeds, fennel seeds, mustard seeds, and turmeric. Bring to a boil, then reduce heat to low and simmer until vegetables are tender but not falling apart, about 1 hour.

3. Remove vegetables and let cool. Place in jars and refrigerate for up to 2 weeks.

Per 1 Cup

Calories: 74 | Fat: 0g | Sodium: 445mg
Carbohydrates: 17g | Fiber: 5g
Sugar: 11g | Protein: 3g

CHOWCHOW

Chowchow is mainly known as a southern food, though a sweeter version of it is also found in Pennsylvania. It wasn't always southern, though. Chowchow migrated with the Acadian people after they were banished from Nova Scotia and settled in Louisiana.

Curried Green Beans

SERVES 5

Green beans taste great just barely cooked and with plenty of snap. But in this instance, you have to cook the beans until they are soft. As the beans break down, they help form the sauce. Serve the beans over steamed rice, ladling the sauce over the top.

Ingredients

2 tablespoons vegetable oil

3 tablespoons red curry paste

6 cups Vegetable Broth
  (see recipe in Chapter 6)

1 pound green beans, trimmed

1. In a large saucepan, heat oil over medium-high heat. Add curry paste and stir-fry for 1 minute.

2. Stir in the Vegetable Broth until well combined with the paste. Add green beans and bring to a low boil. Cook until liquid is reduced, about 15–20 minutes.

3. Reduce the heat to maintain a hard simmer and continue cooking until the beans are very well done, about 15 minutes.

Per Serving

Calories: 95 | Fat: 6g | Sodium: 251mg
Carbohydrates: 9g | Fiber: 3g
Sugar: 3g | Protein: 2g

Chapter Nine

DESSERTS AND DRINKS

Spiced Chocolate Cake

SERVES 10

Serve this spicy, pressure cooker chocolate cake with icing, confectioners' sugar, or vegan ice cream on top.

Ingredients

1½ cups all-purpose flour

4 tablespoons unsweetened cocoa powder

1 teaspoon ground cinnamon

1 teaspoon cayenne pepper

1 teaspoon granulated sugar

¼ teaspoon salt

1 teaspoon baking powder

2 medium bananas, peeled

4 tablespoons vegan margarine, melted

1 cup unsweetened soy milk

2 cups hot water

1. Add the steaming rack to a pressure cooker. Lightly grease an 8" round cake pan with nonstick baking spray.

2. In a medium bowl, mix flour, cocoa powder, cinnamon, cayenne pepper, sugar, salt, and baking powder. In a large bowl, mash the bananas. Add dry ingredients to bananas. Slowly stir in melted margarine and soy milk. Pour the cake mixture into prepared pan.

3. Pour hot water into pressure cooker and set cake pan on rack. Lock the lid into place. Bring to high pressure, then reduce to low and cook for 30 minutes.

4. Remove the pressure cooker from the heat, quick-release the steam, and carefully remove the cake.

Per Serving

Calories: 125 | Fat: 2g | Sodium: 152mg
Carbohydrates: 23g | Fiber: 2g
Sugar: 4g | Protein: 3g

Spiced Peaches

SERVES 6

Spicy and simple to make, these pressure cooker Spiced Peaches will bring a smile to any face.

Ingredients

2 (15-ounce) cans sliced peaches in light syrup

1/4 cup water

1 tablespoon white wine vinegar

1/8 teaspoon allspice

1 medium cinnamon stick

4 whole cloves

1/2 teaspoon ground ginger

1/8 teaspoon cayenne pepper

1 tablespoon minced candied ginger

3 whole peppercorns

1. In a pressure cooker, combine all ingredients and stir to mix. Lock the lid into place and bring to low pressure; maintain pressure for 3 minutes. Remove the pressure cooker from the heat, quick-release the pressure, and remove the lid. Remove and discard the cinnamon stick, cloves, and peppercorns.

2. Return to medium heat. Simmer and stir for 5 minutes to thicken the syrup. Serve warm or chilled. To store, allow to cool and then refrigerate for up to 1 week.

Per Serving

Calories: 80 | Fat: 0g | Sodium: 7mg
Carbohydrates: 22g | Fiber: 2g
Sugar: 19g | Protein: 1g

MAKE SPICED PEACH BUTTER

To make spiced peach butter, after step 2 process the peaches and liquid in a blender or food processor until smooth, and return to the pressure cooker. Simmer and stir over low heat for 30 minutes or until thickened enough to coat the back of a spoon.

Bourbon and Chili Brownies

YIELDS 12 BIG BROWNIES

This recipe yields dense, chewy brownies with spicy hints of chili and bourbon. Sprinkle extra chili powder on top after baking for extra heat.

Ingredients

4 ounces vegan chocolate, roughly chopped

1 stick vegan margarine, softened and cut into small cubes

1 cup granulated sugar

Egg replacer equivalent to 2 eggs

½ teaspoon vanilla extract

¼ cup bourbon

½ cup plus 1 tablespoon all-purpose flour

⅛ teaspoon salt

¼ teaspoon ground cinnamon

½ teaspoon ancho chili powder

1. Preheat oven to 350°F. Grease an 8" square baking pan.

2. In a small microwave-safe bowl, combine chocolate and margarine. Microwave 20 seconds at a time until melted; stir until smooth. (You can also melt the chocolate and margarine in a small saucepan on the stove over low heat.)

3. Transfer chocolate mixture to a large bowl. Add sugar and stir to combine.

4. Add egg replacer and stir until smooth.

5. Add vanilla and bourbon, then stir.

6. Add flour, salt, cinnamon, and chili powder. Stir gently until smooth.

7. Pour mixture into prepared baking pan and bake for 20–25 minutes, until just set in the middle and a toothpick stuck in the center comes out clean.

8. Let brownies cool before cutting.

Per Brownie

Calories: 218 | Fat: 11g | Sodium: 31mg
Carbohydrates: 27g | Fiber: 1g
Sugar: 21g | Protein: 1g

Spicy Fruit Salad

SERVES 4

Tropical fruit sprinkled with chili powder is a popular street snack in Mexico. Consider this a basic guide, and use any amount and combination of fruits or seasonings that you like. It's impossible to screw this up.

Ingredients

½ medium pineapple, peeled, cored, and cut into cubes

1 medium mango, peeled, pitted, and cut into cubes

¼ medium watermelon, peeled and cut into cubes

1 medium papaya, peeled, seeded, and cut into cubes

1 medium jicama, peeled and cut into cubes

1 tablespoon freshly squeezed lime juice

½ teaspoon chili powder

¼ teaspoon salt

1. In a large, shallow bowl, combine all fruit.

2. Squeeze lime juice over fruit. Sprinkle with chili powder and salt, and stir gently to mix ingredients without bruising fruit.

Per Serving

Calories: 322 | Fat: 1g | Sodium: 180mg
Carbohydrates: 81g | Fiber: 15g
Sugar: 55g | Protein: 5g

Mango-Chili Sorbet

SERVES 4

Based on the Mexican fruit-with-chili snack, this plant-based frozen treat is perfect on a hot day. For ultra-smooth ice, purée the mixture two or three times. Or just enjoy it chunky. Serve with an extra sprinkling of chili powder if desired.

Ingredients

8 large mangoes, peeled, pitted, and cut into small cubes

2 cups granulated sugar

3/4 cup freshly squeezed lime juice

1/2 teaspoon ancho chili powder

1. In a blender, combine all ingredients and process until smooth. You may need to add just a little bit of water to achieve the desired consistency.

2. Pour mixture into a large bowl. Cover and put in freezer for 2 hours.

3. Take mixture out of the freezer and purée in blender again.

4. Freeze mixture again until solid.

Per Serving

Calories: 802 | Fat: 2g | Sodium: 17mg
Carbohydrates: 205g | Fiber: 11g
Sugar: 192g | Protein: 6g

MANGOES

Mangoes are a tropical fruit that have been cultivated since as far back as 2000 B.C. in India. Today, they are cultivated throughout Southeast Asia, Mexico, South America, and the Caribbean. Because they continue to ripen even after they are picked, mangoes are a popular export crop and have no trouble making long journeys to their final destinations.

Tamarind Candy

YIELDS 3 CUPS

The combination of spicy, sour, salty, and sweet in a dessert is rare. These candies will keep indefinitely in an airtight jar. You can find concentrated tamarind paste in Asian grocery stores.

Ingredients

2 dried small Thai (bird's eye) chili peppers

$\frac{1}{2}$ teaspoon salt

2 cups concentrated tamarind paste

2 cups tamarind pulp, seeds removed

2 cups granulated sugar, divided

1. Using a mortar and pestle, pound chilies and salt together until they form a powder.

2. In a heavy medium saucepan over low heat, combine tamarind paste, tamarind pulp, $1\frac{1}{2}$ cups sugar, and chili mixture. Stir to mix with a wooden spoon over low heat until thick and sticky, about 5–10 minutes.

3. Remove from heat and let cool. Form mixture into $\frac{1}{2}$" balls and roll in remaining $\frac{1}{2}$ cup sugar. Store in an airtight jar.

Per 1 Cup

Calories: 1,080 | Fat: 1g | Sodium: 2,933mg
Carbohydrates: 274g | Fiber: 17g
Sugar: 239g | Protein: 4g

Bloody Mary Mix

YIELDS ENOUGH FOR 8 BLOODY MARYS

Instead of having to make the same drink over and over again, make a pitcher of this spicy Bloody Mary Mix before having people over for brunch. You can add many types of ingredients to this basic Bloody Mary Mix: raw horseradish, lime juice, wasabi, chili powder, bitters, or anything else you like. Go wild. Combine 2 cups Bloody Mary Mix with 1–2 shots of vodka to make a Bloody Mary.

Ingredients

2 (46-ounce) cans tomato juice

½ cup freshly squeezed lemon juice

2 tablespoons vegan Worcestershire sauce

1 tablespoon horseradish

¼ teaspoon cayenne pepper

½ teaspoon celery salt

½ teaspoon black pepper

1 teaspoon hot sauce

Mix all ingredients and refrigerate.

Per Serving

Calories: 64 | Fat: 0g | Sodium: 958mg
Carbohydrates: 14g | Fiber: 2g
Sugar: 9g | Protein: 3g

Cucumber Margaritas

SERVES 6

Cucumbers offer a mild and cooling contrast in these pretty, light-green drinks. Line the rim with cayenne powder for an extra spicy kick.

Ingredients

2 medium cucumbers, peeled, seeded, and chopped

1/3 cup freshly squeezed lime juice

2 tablespoons superfine sugar

1/2 cup tequila

1/2 teaspoon salt

1/4 teaspoon cayenne pepper

1 cup crushed ice

In blender or food processor, combine cucumbers with remaining ingredients. Cover and blend or process until mixture is smooth and thick.

Per Serving

Calories: 76 | Fat: 0g | Sodium: 196mg
Carbohydrates: 9g | Fiber: 1g
Sugar: 6g | Protein: 1g

Micheladas

SERVES 2

You can vary the ingredients in this classic Mexican drink to your taste. Try it with different kinds of beer too; dark ale will make a more robust Michelada than a light beer.

Ingredients

2 tablespoons freshly squeezed lime juice

¼ teaspoon Tabasco sauce

2 teaspoons vegan Worcestershire sauce

1 tablespoon soy sauce

½ teaspoon salt

2 cups crushed ice

1 (16-ounce) bottle beer

In a cocktail shaker, combine lime juice, Tabasco sauce, Worcestershire sauce, soy sauce, and salt. Shake to blend well. Strain over ice and top with beer, stirring gently to mix.

Per Serving

Calories: 109 | Fat: 0g | Sodium: 1,088mg
Carbohydrates: 11g | Fiber: 0g
Sugar: 1g | Protein: 2g

IN THE LIQUOR STORE

In some liquor stores or grocery stores, you may be able to find a michelada mix to add to cold beer. But the real fun lies in experimenting and adjusting the spices to your liking.

Bloody Maria

SERVES 1

The Bloody Mary goes south of the border with tequila and lime instead of vodka and a celery stalk.

Ingredients

¼ teaspoon celery salt

2 wedges lime

¼ teaspoon vegan Worcestershire sauce

⅛ teaspoon black pepper

1 teaspoon Tabasco sauce

1 ounce tequila

5 ounces tomato juice

1. Spread celery salt on a small plate. Run a lime wedge around the rim of a tall glass, then dip the rim in celery salt.

2. Fill the glass with ice and squeeze the same lime wedge into it.

3. Add celery salt, Worcestershire sauce, pepper, and Tabasco sauce to the glass.

4. Add the tequila and tomato juice and stir well with a bar spoon. Garnish with second lime wedge.

Per Serving

Calories: 90 | Fat: 0g | Sodium: 691mg
Carbohydrates: 6g | Fiber: 1g
Sugar: 4g | Protein: 1g

Mexican Hot Chocolate

SERVES 4

Few things are more comforting on a winter night than a cup of hot chocolate, except this hot chocolate with a little extra spice. Sprinkle more chili powder on top before serving for extra heat.

Ingredients

4 cups unsweetened soy milk

½ cup water

8 ounces vegan semisweet chocolate, finely chopped

2 tablespoons granulated sugar

1 teaspoon vanilla extract

½ teaspoon chili powder

¼ teaspoon ground cinnamon

⅛ teaspoon salt

In a large saucepan over medium heat, combine all ingredients. Whisk constantly until mixture is hot, but not boiling, about 6–8 minutes.

Per Serving

Calories: 410 | Fat: 19g | Sodium: 201mg
Carbohydrates: 49g | Fiber: 5g
Sugar: 39g | Protein: 11g

Hot-Blooded

YIELDS 1 SHOT

There is a common misconception that lighting a shot on fire concentrates the liquor and makes the drink stronger. In reality, lighting the liquor on fire makes the drink less strong. The fire burns away some of the alcohol and weakens the drink.

Ingredients

1½ ounces tequila

2 teaspoons Tabasco sauce

2 tablespoons 151 rum

Pour tequila into a shot glass and add Tabasco sauce. Gently layer the 151 rum on top, then light. Allow the flame to die out before drinking.

Per Shot

Calories: 131 | Fat: 0g | Sodium: 59mg
Carbohydrates: 0g | Fiber: 0g
Sugar: 0g | Protein: 0g

Prairie Fire Shooter

YIELDS 1 SHOT

One taste and you'll understand why they call it fire. You can chase the shooter with a beer to calm the fire.

Ingredients

1½ ounces tequila

3 teaspoons Tabasco sauce

Pour tequila into a shot glass and add Tabasco sauce.

Per Shot

Calories: 99 | Fat: 0g | Sodium: 89mg
Carbohydrates: 0g | Fiber: 0g
Sugar: 0g | Protein: 0g

TEQUILA

Tequila is made from the blue agave, a cactus-like plant that grows in the area near the city of Tequila. True tequila must have a blue agave content of 51 percent; otherwise it is called mescal. Fine tequilas are 100 percent blue agave.

Chocolate Horchata

SERVES 8

This hearty drink is a good start to a cold morning.

Ingredients

½ cup uncooked brown rice

4 cups water

4 cups unsweetened soy milk

2 cups brown sugar

1 teaspoon cayenne pepper

4 ounces unsweetened chocolate, grated

1. In a food processor or blender, grind the rice to a fine powder.

2. In a large saucepan over medium heat, combine rice, water, and soy milk, stirring constantly, until mixture thickens, about 5 minutes. Do not boil.

3. Add brown sugar, cayenne pepper, and grated chocolate. Continue heating, stirring constantly, until mixture produces small bubbles, about 3 minutes. Remove from heat and whip with a hand mixer until frothy.

Per Serving

Calories: 393 | Fat: 8g | Sodium: 78mg
Carbohydrates: 71g | Fiber: 3g
Sugar: 57g | Protein: 7g

US/Metric Conversion Chart

VOLUME CONVERSIONS

US Volume Measure	Metric Equivalent
⅛ teaspoon	0.5 milliliter
¼ teaspoon	1 milliliter
½ teaspoon	2 milliliters
1 teaspoon	5 milliliters
½ tablespoon	7 milliliters
1 tablespoon (3 teaspoons)	15 milliliters
2 tablespoons (1 fluid ounce)	30 milliliters
¼ cup (4 tablespoons)	60 milliliters
⅓ cup	90 milliliters
½ cup (4 fluid ounces)	125 milliliters
⅔ cup	160 milliliters
¾ cup (6 fluid ounces)	180 milliliters
1 cup (16 tablespoons)	250 milliliters
1 pint (2 cups)	500 milliliters
1 quart (4 cups)	1 liter (about)

WEIGHT CONVERSIONS

US Weight Measure	Metric Equivalent
½ ounce	15 grams
1 ounce	30 grams
2 ounces	60 grams
3 ounces	85 grams
¼ pound (4 ounces)	115 grams
½ pound (8 ounces)	225 grams
¾ pound (12 ounces)	340 grams
1 pound (16 ounces)	454 grams

OVEN TEMPERATURE CONVERSIONS

Degrees Fahrenheit	Degrees Celsius
200 degrees F	95 degrees C
250 degrees F	120 degrees C
275 degrees F	135 degrees C
300 degrees F	150 degrees C
325 degrees F	160 degrees C
350 degrees F	180 degrees C
375 degrees F	190 degrees C
400 degrees F	205 degrees C
425 degrees F	220 degrees C
450 degrees F	230 degrees C

BAKING PAN SIZES

American	Metric
8 x 1½ inch round baking pan	20 x 4 cm cake tin
9 x 1½ inch round baking pan	23 x 3.5 cm cake tin
11 x 7 x 1½ inch baking pan	28 x 18 x 4 cm baking tin
13 x 9 x 2 inch baking pan	30 x 20 x 5 cm baking tin
2 quart rectangular baking dish	30 x 20 x 3 cm baking tin
15 x 10 x 2 inch baking pan	30 x 25 x 2 cm baking tin (Swiss roll tin)
9 inch pie plate	22 x 4 or 23 x 4 cm pie plate
7 or 8 inch springform pan	18 or 20 cm spring-form or loose bottom cake tin
9 x 5 x 3 inch loaf pan	23 x 13 x 7 cm or 2 lb narrow loaf or pâté tin
1½ quart casserole	1.5 liter casserole
2 quart casserole	2 liter casserole

Index

EASY PLANT-BASED RECIPES ANYONE CAN MASTER!

THE PLANT-BASED COLLEGE COOKBOOK

Plant-Based, Easy-to-Make, Good-for-You Food

From Tofu Breakfast Burritos to Edamame Pad Thai, 175 Recipes for All of Your Favorites

Pick Up or Download Your Copy Today!